There is hope. 1 ⋯⋯ :I
wish I had known th ⋯⋯ :d
with self-injury for 1. ⋯ ⋯, ⋯⋯ ⋯⋯ ⋯⋯ happy to say that in
2013 I will celebrate five years of being SI-free. This book has encouraged me
much about my own journey. Thank you for writing such an honest yet hopeful
perspective on self-injury. I wish I had known this stuff a long time ago. Perhaps
then it would not have taken me over thirty years to find freedom.

—Julia (Ajax, Ontario)

The Wounding Embrace touches on an area that the Church has shied
away from for many years. People who cut aren't "damaged" and need to be
fixed; they don't need to pray harder or be more "Christian." They need to
be understood. As someone who has struggled with cutting in the Christian
circle, this book is a breath of fresh air. Finally, someone gets it. Hopefully
this book will enable not only church leaders, but others as well, to come
alongside individuals struggling with self-harm and understand the problem
so they can grasp why self-injurers struggle and be able to support them to
end the cycle.

—Jamie (Pickering, Ontario)

This book is a great read for people in all situations of self-injury, whether
they are the self-injurer or the confidant. Brett provides many resources for
those suffering through this pain and helps in making sense of self-injury. "In
the Therapist's Office" shatters our preconceived ideas about counselling and
gives us hope. As someone who used to cut, all I can say is this: Don't give up.
God has so much more planned for you than you could ever imagine. Brett
has helped me over the years and I'm confident this book will provide hope,
motivation, and healing for you as well.

—Arial (Manitoba)

As someone who struggles with cutting, I thought the book was very
empowering. Brett Ullman is non-judgmental and is able to explain why I cut.
I now feel as though I'm not alone and that people actually understand why I
do it, instead of the people in my life who I've hid this from. I especially loved
the therapist sessions. Since reading this book, I have not self-harmed and I'd
like to keep it that way.

—Natasha (Ajax, Ontario)

The Wounding Embrace takes self-injury, an issue that's too often stereotyped and misunderstood, and lays out the accurate facts about it in an easily understandable format. Brett addresses the common misconceptions of self-injury, talks about what it really looks like, and presents solutions. As a former self-injurer, it's very encouraging to read a book like this. One of the toughest things I remember from when I was cutting was that no one understood why I would choose to help myself in that way. *The Wounding Embrace* shows self-injurers that they can be understood and that there is hope and healing available. It also opens the eyes of non-self-injurers to this issue.

—*Harmony (Red Deer, Alberta)*

As an adult who self-injured for many years, I found the message of hope in this book to be not only comforting, but also truthful. I applaud Brett Ullman for encouraging people to open the lines of communication and get involved in the lives of those who are struggling. I assure you that if I felt I could talk about my problems and not be judged, but loved, I would have stopped harming myself much sooner.

—*Leigh-Anne (London, Ontario)*

For many years, I was in a place described in this book, a place of fear and shame governed by self-injury. *The Wounding Embrace* is a powerful, practical tool that I know will help set people free from damaging thoughts and actions, and Brett's compassion and empathy are evident on every page. By the end, we are left with more than just a great tool or resource—we are left with hope.

—*Adam (Grand Rapids, Michigan)*

YOUR STORY:
The Wounding Embrace

Brett Ullman & Adam Clarke
with contributions by Dr. Merry C Lin

Worlds Apart Series - Book 3

Printed in Canada

ISBN: 978-1-77069-891-8

Word Alive Press
131 Cordite Road, Winnipeg, MB R3W 1S1
www.wordalivepress.ca

Library and Archives Canada Cataloguing in Publication

Ullman, Brett, 1971-
        The wounding embrace : your story / Brett Ullman and Adam Clarke.
ISBN 978-1-77069-891-8

        1. Teenagers--Mental health. 2. Adolescent psychopathology.
I. Clarke, Adam, 1984- II. Title.

RJ503.U55 2013   616.8900835   C2013-901836-0

To all my fellow journeyers searching for hope and healing.

Table of Contents

"I may not be strong enough to stop now, but now I don't feel so alone. We sat in the front row and a girl came up to me. She just smiled and said 'we match.' I saw the cuts on her arms that resembled mine and felt a rush of understanding. She didn't tell me I was crazy like the kids at school, and she didn't look down on me, thinking I wanted to commit suicide, like my mom thought. This girl knew what I was going through. I just wanted to thank you for sharing your message and giving me that opportunity to realize that I'm not alone in my battle."

—*Samm*

"When I was in recovery, I decided to live instead of living my life dying."

—*Brittany*

Foreword

This book is for anyone who's struggling with self-injury, or for anyone who knows someone who is struggling. Some sections will be for youth leaders and teachers, others will be for friends and family members who know someone who is struggling, and still others will be for those who are wrestling with self-injury.

I hope this book can be the start of a healing process for any of the above groups as they look to move forward from the shackles of self-injury.

The stories you'll find throughout this book come from The Wounding Embrace website (www.yourstory.info), and emails that have been sent to me by students, young adults, middle-aged parents, and even some seniors whose lives have been impacted by self-injury. I hope their stories can inspire hope that there is a bright light at the end of this dark path.

Introduction

When I first began this conversation with students and youth workers, many people told me I couldn't do it. One lady came up to me after I announced to a crowd that if they came back to the same stage the next day, I would be speaking about cutting and suicide. This woman made a beeline towards me. Next thing I knew, she was right up in my face, talking rather quickly at me.

"Brett, you can't."

"Can't what?" I asked.

"You can't talk about cutting and suicide. I brought this large group down and if you talk about cutting and suicide, they're all going to go home and cut and kill themselves."

To which I very inappropriately burst out laughing. Who would believe that? I quickly realized she actually did. The only reply I could muster was, "What?"

This weighed on me that night in my hotel. Maybe it was just me. Maybe I receive so many letters from young students merely because I'm an easy target. I come into their schools and I'm an easy person to email because there's no face to look into as they write and share. The accountability factor is removed. Maybe this woman was right. Maybe

I was just enhancing and enabling the very actions I was there to speak out against.

That night, I made a decision: I would have to follow up by asking the audience how many of them knew someone who struggled with cutting, bulimia, anorexia, suicide, or any other form of self-injury.

When I did this, I couldn't believe the response. I thought that it would be a majority, but I wasn't expecting ninety percent of the thousand people in attendance to raise their hands.

Ask yourself that question right now. Do you know someone who struggles with anorexia? Bulimia? Depression? Cutting? Suicide?

I know these are dark thoughts and many of us don't want to think about them. But as you list names in your head, the importance of this discussion should become clear. I would also encourage anyone who's approaching this book with a faith background to take those names and add them into your journal, Google doc, or Evernote folder so you can pray for them everyday.

This conversation isn't just for students in junior high or high school; it's not just for young adults, either. Self-injury has become a life problem. I say a life problem because it doesn't matter if I'm speaking to junior high, high school, or young adults; the same ninety percent always know people who are struggling. When I ask parents the same question, it's closer to fifty percent. We'll dive into numbers and statistics a bit later, but for right now I would like to speak practically.

After this speaking engagement, I attended The Global Leadership Summit,[1] a conference that is broadcast by satellite, aimed at creating better leaders in all areas of life. At the summit, Bill Hybels and Rick Warren challenged me to what they call "feeding your holy discontent." As I went home that night, I wrote down three things that really bug me in this world:

1) AIDS.

2) How the church treats the homosexual community.

3) Cutting.

---

1 Willow Creek Association. "The Global Leadership Summit." Date of Access: April 2012 (http://www.willowcreek.com/events/leadership/).

I sat at home thinking about how I could contribute my time to these three areas. As I came up with strategic and practical ways I could feed my discontents, I couldn't help but keep coming back to one singular thought regarding my discontent with cutting: "What can I do?"

I don't come from a background of depression or self-injury, yet this topic has always weighed heavily on my heart. My next step was to go to Amazon and buy every book I could find on self-injury. I opened that first book and began to read, and as I read I began to remember. I remembered one of my first years as a teacher, when I kicked a girl out of class and she returned a short time later with the broken beer bottle she had used to carve up her face, arms, and chest. No teachers college program could ever prepare you for that.

As this flood of memory came back to me, I began to remember more examples of self-injury in my background. I remembered a young girl who passed away from anorexia, a girl I had trained while working as a fitness trainer back in university. I realized this was part of the man I had become because of the toll it had taken on the people in my life.

So why am I writing this book?

I'm writing this book to start a discussion. Some of us already have these discussions, but for the most part they happen in very small circles. All of us, like myself, have been affected in one way or another by self-injury. If we can get a discussion going, we can provide a safe place for these individuals to confide in us a very powerful secret. We may be invited into a person's secret life, but we also have to be ready and willing to join in their recovery, in whatever ways they need. We can then help them down the path to recovery.

IN THE THERAPIST'S OFFICE
Introduction

THROUGHOUT THIS BOOK ARE EXCERPTS WRITTEN FROM THE PERSPECTIVE of fictional psychotherapy sessions with Dr. Merry Lin, a real-life psychologist. My hope is these sessions can help debunk the myths people have about what happens in a therapist's office. It is my strong belief that many times we need someone trustworthy to walk with, to hear our stories and help us break free from the pain and fear that hold us back.

Many times, we have wrong conceptions of what happens in therapy, as we fear being judged or we battle with secret shame. Many of us keep secrets close to our chests, and we feel like there's no hope. But it's been my experience that there is great value in seeing a trusted and competent Christian psychotherapist, counsellor, or psychologist who is skilled and compassionate, someone who can help you navigate the journey of healing. Please read these excerpts with an open mind and heart. My prayer is that you will experience hope in the possibility that your story *can* change.

These sessions demonstrate the main phases of therapy. First comes the beginning, during which therapeutic trust and safety is established. The next phase involve psycho-educational sessions which help clients understand some of the physiological and psychological underpinnings of cutting, depression, anxiety, and eating disorders. Next comes sessions which focus on learning coping strategies to keep oneself grounded and safe despite great emotional turmoil. Following that, the patient typically undergoes a variety of trauma recovery therapies, many of which are non-verbal, as many traumatized clients, particularly teens, find it difficult to talk about their experiences; they therefore find it helpful to use creative means to express their pain and tell their stories. Patients also develop mechanisms to regulate their emotions, tolerate distress, and develop a sense of confidence in their ability to stay resilient regardless of what happens.

One final disclaimer before we get going. Dr. Lin has consolidated these sessions into twelve parts. However, the healing journey often takes place over months—and sometimes even years, depending on the complexity of the issues and depth of trauma that has occurred.

ONE
Bridging the Pain

How will you know when I'm hurting
If you cannot see my pain?
To wear it on my body
Tells what words cannot explain.[2]
—C. Blount

It's a problem rarely discussed, even though millions struggle with it, usually beginning in adolescence. And because no one talks about it, many believe they are suffering alone.[3]
—Dateline

n o issue in our world today brings up more emotional feelings than self-harm. Henri Nouwen, one of my favourite authors, says, "Our life is full of brokenness… How can we live with that brokenness without becoming bitter and resentful except by returning

---

2 Conterio, Karen, Wendy Lader, and Jennifer K. Bloom. *Bodily Harm: The Break-through Treatment Program for Self-Injurers* (New York, NY: Hyperion, 1998), p. xi.

3 Statics: Issues. "Transcript: Dateline." Date of Access: August 2, 2012 (http://www.static8.com/issues/tscript_dl.html).

again and again to God's faithful presence in our lives?"[4] As a Christian (a follower of the Way), do I believe God can heal?

Yes, I do.

Do you?

Do I believe God is present, in our healing? Yes.

Again, do you?

I will, however, part ways with the faith questions for a moment, because this is what I hear all the time: "Brett, I talked to my pastor, I talked to my youth leader, I talked to my whoever, and I told them I'm struggling with cutting. Their response was to pray to Jesus and you will be fine." Is the "pray to Jesus" answer appropriate, or is it just an easy answer?

I acknowledge that God can heal, but let me also say that the "pray to Jesus" answer, to me, is religious abuse. We are called to be the hands and feet of God.

> *The way God designed our bodies is a model for understanding our lives together as a church: every part dependent on every other part, the parts we mention and the parts we don't, the parts we see and the parts we don't. If one part hurts, every other part is involved in the hurt, and in the healing. If one part flourishes, every other part enters into the exuberance.*
> (1 Corinthians 12:25–26)

If you or someone you know is hurting because they cut or harm themselves, and you've heard the "pray to Jesus" answer, I'm sorry. We're all called to stand beside each other, care for each other, and help heal one another. But we don't. We walk away over and over again. Too often we simply walk away.

So yes, I acknowledge my faith, but how do we be the hands and feet of God?

Healing is like building a bridge. No one person needs to bridge the whole hurt, because that's too much for one person to handle. I believe

---

4 Nouwen, Henri. *Sabbatical Journey: The Diary of His Final Year* (New York, NY: Crossroad Publishers, 1998), p. 134.

God helps us with that bridge; if we start the bridge, he will finish it. That's the component I think we forget about. If someone who's dealing with any form of self-injury approaches you, God has directed guided that person to you for a reason. Allow God to work through you and into their life.

IN THE THERAPIST'S OFFICE

Session One: by Dr. Merry Lin

YOU WALK INTO THE SHRINK'S OFFICE FOR THE FIRST TIME, FURIOUS AT YOUR parents for making you come. You wish they would just leave you alone! You're determined to say nothing, because you're sick and tired of all these adults judging you and telling you what to do. What more can this doctor tell you that you haven't already heard? Bunch of freaking shrinks shoving pills at you and telling you to stop it. They just don't get it and they never will. No one ever does. They don't know anything about you.

You slump down in the chair, shoulders hunched and head down, arms hidden and tucked into the sleeves of your shirt. Your heart is pounding, even while you're trying hard to pretend like you don't care. You feel like you might have a panic attack right there and then, but that would be the worst thing, so you tell yourself to stay strong until you get home, where you can take care of yourself in the only way you know how. You grit your teeth and hope the shrink will get the vibe that you don't want to be there and maybe somehow leave you alone. Fat chance.

I look at you, and I see you. I smile at you even as you refuse to look me in the eye. But that's okay; you don't have to look at me. You don't have to say anything out loud because I can hear you. I can hear your silent screams. My heart breaks at all the things you can't say out loud but desperately wish someone would hear. I hear you. You have a voice with me.

I know it's going to take some time for you to trust me and that's okay. I know that you'll do a bunch of things to push me away or test me, and that's okay, too. I'm not going anywhere. I know you don't believe me yet, but I won't judge you. I actually like you just as you are, as prickly or withdrawn as you can be. I see you and hear your pain. I want to hear your story. I know it's going to take time, but I'm going to walk with you, and together we're going to make sure that you'll be okay. More than okay. Why, you ask? Because I believe in you.

I tell you right up front about confidentiality, and remind you that I won't be talking about our sessions with anyone, not even your parents. This is supposed to be your safe place to say whatever you want without worrying about it coming back to bite you. I let you know that the only time I'll ever break confidentiality is if you tell me you're suicidal or you're seriously thinking of harming someone else, but even then, I promise that I will let you know about what I'm going to say and do. I tell you that even if your parents call to talk about their concerns, they'll be told that you're going to hear about their phone call. Nothing will be said behind your back, because this is your deal, not theirs. This is about helping you.

Today, I'm not going to ask you a bunch of questions about your story because I know it will unfold throughout our time together. I'm not going to ask you questions you can't answer, because if you knew the answers to these questions, you wouldn't be here. I'm more interested in hearing about you—what you like and don't like, your friends, music, school, family, etc. I want to get to know you. You're so worth getting to know. And the more I get to know you, the more I like you. I'm going to enjoy hanging out with you.

You don't get it. Why isn't she asking about the cutting? Why isn't she spouting off all her expert advice to get you to stop? You're feeling suspicious but intrigued in spite of yourself. You find yourself relaxing— you can do this, just talking about your life. Before you know it, the fifty minutes have quickly passed. That wasn't so bad. The shrink was actually kind of nice. She didn't ask any of those stupid questions adults ask. You like the way she laughs and smiles at what you have to say, and you enjoy seeing the warmth in her eyes. You feel accepted by her.

When she starts telling you that she likes you and has really enjoyed hanging out with you, you feel kind of weird. You start to feel warm and soft on the inside but scared at the same time, with a little bit of suspicion as well. Why would she say that? What kind of doctor is she anyway? And when she talks about being on your side and that you have a voice with her, you have to fight back tears. They trickle down your face anyway and you swipe them away, hoping she didn't notice. You're afraid to believe her, but somewhere in your heart a tiny feeling of hope begins to flicker. You fight to keep your face impassive; you're still not sure you can trust her, but maybe you'll give this therapy thing a chance. See where it goes.

TWO
Cutting

When we think of self-injury, we think of "cutting." In reality, though, that's a slang term. Too often it's thrown around with little regard for the feelings of those suffering from the condition.

In emergency rooms, people with self-inflicted wounds are often told directly and indirectly that they are not as deserving of care as someone who has an accidental injury. They are treated badly by the same doctors who would not hesitate to do everything possible to preserve the life of an overweight, sedentary heart-attack patient.[5]

Sufferers have traditionally been met with disgust by doctors, who find their self-injuring offensive. Therapists are often unwelcoming too, mistakenly labeling such people suicidal or dismissing them as "borderline," a catchall category for manipulative, difficult patients with intractable disorders.

---

5 Self-Injury.org. "Self-Injury: A Quick Guide to the Basics." Date of Access: February 2012 (http://www.selfinjury.org/docs/factsht.html).

In reality… cutters are people frozen in trauma. More than half of self-injurers are victims of sexual abuse, and most report emotionally abusive or neglected childhoods, the strains of which send them into an emotional grave.[6]

Borderlines are characterized in Karen Conterio's book *Bodily Harm* as sufferers "characterized by their rapid mood swings, difficulty maintaining friendships, emotional sensitivity, and impulse problems."[7] However, the reality is much different than what you'll hear from doctors and therapists.

People who cut are frozen in the trauma of their lives. I spoke to a young girl from Durham who told me about her experience with a doctor. She walked into the hospital with her arm bleeding. After she was tended to, she received a very chilling warning: "If you ever do it again, we're going to stitch you up without anaesthetic." How would you have responded to that doctor if you had been with that young girl?

Steven Levenkron says this in *Cutting: Understanding and Overcoming Self-Mutilation*:

> The act of deliberately causing oneself to bleed frightens us in many complicated and varied ways. Clearly, people who harm or inadvertently kill themselves create in us a very uncomfortable mix of fear, guilt, anger, and frustration
>
> In order to understand and treat self-mutilators, we have to understand enough about ourselves so that we can become effective in helping those who feel abandoned, without confusing our own fears with theirs. [8]

6 Time Magazine. "What the Cutters Feel." Date of Access: April 2012 (http://www.time.com/time/magazine/article/0,9171,140405,00.html).

7 Conterio, Karen, Wendy Lader, and Jennifer Kingson Bloom. *Bodily Harm: The Breakthrough Treatment Program for Self-Injurers* (New York, NY: Hyperion, 1998), p. 18.

8 Levenkron, Steven. *Cutting: Understanding and Overcoming Self-Mutilation.* (New York, NY: W.W. Norton, 1998), p. 21.

The majority of you, as readers, may be in this situation. We are all trying to cope with our emotions towards this topic, as well as trying to understand the emotions of the self-injurers in our lives.

Self-harm is not a failed suicide attempt.

In *A Bright Red Scream: Self-Mutilation and the Language of Pain*, author Marilee Strong explains the hidden life that is found in cutting oneself:

> Cutting is really a remarkable, ingenious solution to the problem of "not existing." It provides concrete, irrefutable proof that one is alive.[9]

For many of these sufferers, cutting themselves proves that they are, indeed, part of the very world that is shutting them out.

> "There is a hazy line," says Lindsay, a fifteen-year-old cutter. "If I'm suicidal I want to die, I have lost all hope. When I'm self-injuring, I want to relieve emotional pain and keep on living. Suicide is a permanent exit. Self-injury helps me get through the moment."[10]

Like Lindsay, most cutters aren't looking to gain attention from those around them, but attempting to cope with what they're going through.

> Cutting is not attention seeking. It's not manipulative. It's a coping mechanism—a punitive, unpleasant, potentially dangerous one—but it works. It helps me cope with strong emotions that I don't know how to deal with. Don't tell me I'm sick, don't tell me to stop. Don't try to make me feel guilty, that's how I feel already. Listen to me, support me, help me.[11]

---

9 Strong, Marilee. *A Bright Red Scream: Self-Mutilation and the Language of Pain.* (New York, NY: Viking, 1998), p. 55.

10 Ibid., p. 32.

11 Ibid., p. 2.

I find that I learn more about self-injury when the stories and quotes I hear come directly from those who are being affected by self-injury. These stories and emails invite me into their lives, their struggles, and their search for life outside self-injury.

Melissa and Andrea are two girls who have emailed me their stories. I have walked alongside them at different points in their struggles and successes. According to them, self-injury is *not* a suicide attempt. It's a way of making emotional pain into something physical that you can see and control. Melissa sees her pain through cutting and feels it helps to control the pain. Andrea told me, "Self-injury keeps me alive, simple as that."

So, what is it? Self-harm, self-injury… you can call it either one, but do not call it self-mutilation. Self-mutilation is a totally different thing where people mutilate their bodies merely for the sake of mutilating their bodies.

There is a definition for self-injury. It goes like this:

> Self-injury is the act of deliberately harming your own body, such as cutting or burning yourself. It's not meant as a suicide attempt. Rather, self-injury is an unhealthy way to cope with emotional pain, intense anger and frustration.[12]

For me, I define it as hurting yourself in any way, shape, or form with anything you can imagine to get beyond overwhelming feelings, thoughts, or emotions.

In the last couple of decades, the media has begun to pick up on this topic. Shows like *7th Heaven* and *Degrassi* have aired episodes centred on this topic. Self-injury has even started showing up in dozens and dozens of movies.

Another area of the media that has touched on this topic is the music industry. I can remember when the Goo Goo Dolls released a song in which they cried out, "Just to bleed to know you're alive."[13]

12 Mayo Clinic. "Self-Injury/Cutting." Date of Access: August 8, 2012 (http://www.mayoclinic.com/health/self-injury/DS00775)

13 Goo Goo Dolls. "Dizzy Up the Girl." Burbank, CA: Warner Bros, 1998.

Other songs have touched on the theme more substantially, such as Papa
Roach's *Last Resort*:

Cut my life into pieces
I've reached my last resort
Suffocation
No breathing
Don't give a f*** if I cut my arm bleeding
Do you even care if I die bleeding?
Do you even care if I die bleeding?
Who did me wrong?
Who did me right?
If I took my life tonight
Chances are that I might
Mutilation outta sight
And I'm contemplating suicide[14]

This song went double platinum and spent time at the very top of
the charts. I find this fascinating, because this is the number one song I
get emails about. The emails say, "I self-injure to this song." For them,
the song is a trigger that could set them off, even if they just hear it
randomly on the radio.

Razor, by the Foo Fighters, is another one of these theme songs.
In it, Dave Growl sings solo with a guitar, almost peacefully trying to
come to grips with the relationship the razor and the guitar seem to
have.

Wake up it's time
We need to find a better place to hide
Make up your mind
I need to know I need to know tonight

Sweet and divine
Razor of mine

14 Papa Roach. "Last Resort." Beverly Hills, CA: Dreamworks Records, 2000.

Sweet and divine
Razorblade shine[15]

You get the feeling the object has a hold on the owner that even the owner doesn't understand. He wants to break away, but he's constantly drawn back no matter how well he thinks the has hidden. I get chills from the reality of this song. The key to the song is the idea that the best way to cope with self-injury is to remove the object that causes the hurt. The act of cutting is a coping mechanism, but the goal should be to cope with emotions and feelings through other means. There are other coping strategies.

> They're training wheels, and they teach you that you can get through a crisis without hurting yourself. You can refine them; even devise more productive coping mechanisms, later. Use these to demonstrate to yourself that you can cope without permanently injuring your body.[16]

If removing the objects we cut with is too difficult, creating more stress and anxiety, then a coping strategy like holding ice might be the first step towards not hurting yourself.

The truth is that people self-harm in different ways. Cutting is the most common method, but there are hundreds others.

Types of SI	Types of SI
Cutting and similar	Breaking bones
Burning	Eating disorders
Banging your head	Punching or throwing yourself against hard objects
Not allowing cuts to heal	Ingesting poison or foreign objects

---

15 Foo Fighters. "Razor." New York, NY: Roswell Records, 2005.

16 "Self-Mutilation/Cutting." Date of Access: February 2012 (http://web.archive.org/web/20030106003206/http://www.i-p-d.com/safehaven/libcut.htm).

Types of SI	Types of SI
Binge drinking	Overdosing on drugs
Piercing your skin with foreign objects	Pulling out your hair

The fact that you self-injure doesn't mean you're crazy.

Self-injury is a sign of distress not madness; a sign of someone trying to cope with life as best [he or she] can.[17]

At this point in the book, or even at this point during one of my talks, people in the crowd are usually looking around and thinking the same thing: *I just don't get it. How can someone take a razor and cut themselves?*

The following analogy has helped me understand and answer that question.

Imagine it's winter and you are staying at a cabin with your family. The cabin is by a river, and when you look out the window at the river, you see that it's pristine. The water is calm and smooth with no imperfections, almost like a sheet of glass has been laid out over it. As you go outside, you realize that it *is* a sheet of glass—or rather, a thick layer of ice. As you make your way out onto the ice, your three-year-old son runs out ahead of you and, boom, crashes through the ice into the water.

As a parent, or even as a bystander, I would hope your next instinct would be to get into the water and pull them to safety.

But what is the goal in that situation? Is it to rescue the child, or is it to experience the cold water? Will the water be cold? Yes, but the goal is to rescue the child.

When someone cuts him or herself, the goal is not the act of cutting. The goal is the endorphin release that comes after you're done. Just like the goal of grabbing your child out of the water isn't to get cold, the goal

---

17 Bristol Crisis Service for Women. "Women and self-injury." Date of Access: March 2012 (http://www.users.zetnet.co.uk/BCSW/leaflets/womensa.htm).

of cutting isn't cutting yourself. The end product is what matters, not the act itself.

This brings up an interesting question.

> If a person proceeds despite the pain, that means that he or she is motivated by something stronger than the pain, something that makes him or her capable of ignoring or enduring it. It takes intense feelings to ignore pain.[18]

There needs to be intense feelings for someone to ignore the pain, because no one likes to be in pain. So, what is causing those intense feelings and how do we help self-injurers address them in a safe and appropriate manner?

According to an article I read in Time Magazine, people cut for one of two reasons: to feel more, or to feel less.[19] There's either too much going on in their lives, emotionally, or there's a disconnect of emotions in their lives.

We need to look at the reasons people harm themselves. It can be a coping mechanism; someone can cut in order to cope with whatever situation is going on. In this sense, cutting provides a sense of relief. The reality is that we, as humans, feel. We feel too much, we feel too little, and when it gets really bad sometimes we do not feel at all. When we do not feel at all, we become numb, and being numb is scary, because at that point our bodies simply shut down. The problem then such a person cannot feel happy anymore, or love, or show compassion; their body has shut down all emotion in order to keep from getting hurt again. However, they continue to search for ways to release the tension that builds up inside. The tension relief becomes the act of cutting, which is the coping mechanism to being numb, or emotionally overwhelmed.

---

18 Levenkron, Steven. *Cutting: Understanding and Overcoming Self-Mutilation.* (New York, NY: W.W. Norton, 1998), p. 41.

19 Time Magazine. "What the Cutters Feel." Date of access: April 2012 (http://www.time.com/time/magazine/article/0,9171,140405,00.html).

Some other reasons can be that we want to feel the hurt on the outside and not on the inside, we want to become unattractive (undesirable) so that we do not get hurt, or perhaps we want to regain control when we feel like we're out of control, whether it be at work, home, church, or school. I hear a new reason every time I get an email or have coffee with someone who is struggling with this.

The number one reason that self-injury occurs is that people do it to stay alive. Candy was sixteen when she wrote:

> When I was in sixth grade, my father died, and things got much worse. My mother was too depressed to really notice my depression and the rest of my family never really noticed either. Emotions you would not believe built up inside of me the same year my grandmother died.[20]

Emotions are tricky to figure out during adolescence because our cognitive development is still occurring. Our ability to process and deal with emotions is still being developed. The emotions take over, forcing teenagers to find ways to cope.

Many of these sufferers see self-injury as a way to cope with their feelings without involving, hurting, or even offending those closest to them. My question for all of us would be this: what have we done to these individuals to make them feel like they cannot be honest with us about what they're dealing with? We are called to be the hands and feet of Jesus, to show him to the world through our actions and words. So, why do so many sufferers feel like they need to cope alone? Anyone who goes through a wide range of emotions when they engage in self-injury think they have made a mistake; that realization takes them through a process of emotional responses that leads them right back to injuring themselves.

> I have made a mistake. I am so angry with myself. God, why am I so stupid? How can I be so bad? I am so worthless. I

---

20 S.T.O.R.M Texas. "Self-Harm Info." Date of Access: August 8, 2012 (http://stormtx. wordpress.com/sismsh-stats-info/self-harm-info/).

don't deserve to be happy. I want to punish myself. I am a bad person. I want to cut myself.[21]

This cycle of responses will continue until the underlying emotions are addressed.

The necessity to identify, challenge, and alter each negative thought that you have cannot be denied. Changing your thoughts will help you to change your behaviours, emotions, and physical sensations and will help you to decrease your desires to hurt yourself.[22]

We'll go into more detail about the self-injury cycle later.

The truth is that lots of people self-harm. A man actually yelled out at one of my talks, "Why would you ever talk about this?" When I flipped my slide, he quietly sat back down in his seat.

An article in The Lancet from June 2012 shows that there is strong evidence that self-harm amongst young adolescents is on the rise.

Self-harm presentations become increasingly common from age 12 years onwards, particularly in girls, such that between ages 12 years and 15 years the girl-to-boy ratio is as high as five or six to one.[23]

In a self-injury prevalence study conducted by Act For Youth Centre of Excellence, with collaborations from Cornell University, Rochester University, and the New York State Centre for School Safety, entitled

---

21 Washington Parent. "A Cry for Help: What Parents of Teens Need to Know About Cutting." Date of Access: January 2012 (http://washingtonparent.com/articles/0502/cutting.html).

22 Self-Injury.net. "How to Stop Hurting Yourself." Date of Access: February 2012 (http://self-injury.net/information-recovery/recovery/how-stop-hurting-yourself).

23 The Lancet. "Self-harm and suicide in adolescents." Date of Access: June 23, 2012 (http://www.thelancet.com/journals/lancet/article/PIIS0140-6736(12)60322-5/fulltext#article_upsell).

The Cutting Edge: Non-Suicidal Self-Injury in Adolescence, found that the number has grown from one in six in 2008 to almost one in four only a year later.

> In general, studies suggest that about 13% to 25% of adolescents and young adults surveyed in schools have some history of self-injury (Rodham & Hawton, 2009). However, many of these young people engage in self-injury once or twice, then stop. Others become chronic self-injurers. Studies of self-injury in college populations suggest that about 6% of the college population are actively and chronically self-injuring, while many more have some history of self- injury. While there are no analogous statistics for adolescent populations, prevalence is likely to be roughly similar. Middle school populations may have somewhat higher prevalence since that is the age at which most individuals initiate self- injury. (Whitlock, Eckenrode, et al., 2006; Gollust, Eisenberg, & Golberstein, 2008). [24]

This is a growing issue that needs to be addressed, because people who are unfamiliar with self-harm and why it's happening have a very skewed opinion on the subject.

One of the first things I hear when I talk about this subject with teens is, "Yeah, I know that kid. They're emo." If you're over the age of forty, you might use the word "goth." Both are used to describe the fashion sense of a common type of self-abuser. These types are not identical or interchangeable with one another, of course. If you think the only person who struggles with self-harm wears black, you're just wrong. There is no "that" person. There is no particular nationality. There is no one ethnicity. Age doesn't even matter, because anyone can struggle with self-injury. The youngest person I have dealt with was in Grade Three and the oldest was a seventy-seven-year-old. Self-injury doesn't pick and choose.

---

24 Whitlock, Janis. *The Cutting Edge: Non-Suicidal Self-Injury in Adolescents*. Research Facts and Findings, December 2009. Date of Access: March 2012 (http://www.actfory-outh.net/resources/rf/rf_nssi_1209.cfm).

It's really hard to narrow down a specific type of person who self-injures, but as research continues we are discovering that the majority of self-injurers are female. Karen Conterio, in *Bodily Harm*, describes what she calls the typical sufferer.

> The "typical" self-injurer, if there is one, would be white, middle-class woman of above-average intelligence who began cutting herself in adolescence. She has low self-esteem and may suffer from bouts of depression. She has trouble relating to people and forming intimate relationships...[25]

She also describes the typical adolescent childhood of a person who self-injures this way:

> Many were physically, sexually, or emotionally abused, or had parents who ignored their basic needs. Many are children of alcoholics or mentally ill people who neglected and tormented them. Most grew up in rigid households where expressions of emotion were quashed and religious or military-style thinking ruled the day, or where their every move was scrutinized and criticized by a hovering and intrusive parent. On the other end of the spectrum, some self-injurers grew up in homes where there was little, or no parental guidance or emotional involvement.[26]

As I read both of those descriptions, I couldn't help but realize how typical they are. How many of those environmental factors are evident in today's households? Think about it for a moment. Parents who are emotionally distant? They don't need to be alcoholics or mentally ill, but let's say they give their smart phones more attention than their child. Also, when they give their kids the attention they're looking for, it is in an overprotective and intrusive manner. Add in the typical female

---

25 Conterio, Karen, Wendy Lader, and Jennifer K. Bloom. *Bodily Harm: The Breakthrough Treatment Program for Self-Injurers.* (New York, NY: Hyperion, 1998), p. 19.

26 Ibid.

self-injurer description and you have probably included the majority of all junior high school students you know. They're struggling with the questions like "Who am I?" and "What is my place in the world?" and "How can I become accepted by my peer group?"

Almost every junior high school student can fit into that description. That's what makes pinpointing a self-injurer so difficult. It's all in how they learn to cope with their emotions and how they view themselves. Studies are beginning to come out that suggest teaching kids to cope with emotional stress while in school may be the best solution to the growing number of kids who deal with self-injury.

> This study examined the effectiveness of a universal school-based prevention program that was designed to increase coping resources in preadolescents through the modeling and teaching of optimistic thinking skills. School psychologists, together with classroom teachers, implemented an eight-week program in eight Year 5 and 6 class groups as part of the regular school curricula. One hundred and sixty children who participated in the program were compared to 135 children in 8 control groups on pre- and post-test questionnaires. Post-test responses show that children who participated in the program reported significant improvements in coping efficacy, and reductions in depressive attributions and use of the non-productive coping strategies of worry, wishful thinking, not coping, and ignoring the problem when compared to controls. These results support the feasibility of implementing low-cost, non-intrusive programs in school settings that address the emotional health of all young people. Support is also provided for theories that suggest attributions for events and coping efficacy influence the selection of coping strategies.[27]

---

27 Cornell Research Program on Self-Injurious Behaviour in Adolescents and Young Adults. "Coping Research." Date of Access: July 2012 (http://www.crpsib.com/userfiles/File/Annotated%20Bib%20Coping.pdf).

There's no question that self-injury is not an individual problem. The skills needed to cope with these confusing emotions aren't possible for just anyone entering adolescence; they need every caring adult in their lives to teach them the skills needed to navigate adolescence successfully.

IN THE THERAPIST'S OFFICE
Session Two: by Dr. Merry Lin

YOU SIT IN THE WAITING ROOM, FEELING KIND OF WEIRD. YOU FEEL ANTSY AND nervous, but in some strange way you're also kind of looking forward to seeing the shrink. You wonder if she'll be as nice as she was last week. But you still don't know what to make of her. She's not what you expected, so maybe you read the situation wrong. She doesn't seem like most of the doctors you've met before, but you're still suspicious that maybe this week she'll start trying to fix you and tell you what to do. You're not sure what to expect, so you sit there, jiggling your leg nervously as you wait. You play with your phone, mindlessly texting your friends to pass the time while you wait. Hurry up already.

She comes out of her office and greets you with a warm smile. You can't help but smile back, because she actually seems glad to see you. Go figure. You follow her into her office and slump down in the same chair, not sure what to say or do. You cross your arms and look at her, waiting. She starts chattering away about a wild turkey that apparently attacked one of the cars in the parking lot and you can't help but laugh as you hear the story. What the heck? You still don't know what to make of her, but you find yourself relaxing as she tells the story.

You watch as she starts to spread all these magazines on the table and hands you a pair of scissors and some glue. She tells you to flip through the magazines and just pick out any pictures that catch your interest and then glue them all together on a big piece of paper to make a collage. It wasn't what you expected to do with the shrink, but okay, whatever, you can do this. As you cut and paste, you find yourself telling her about your week. She really seems to listen and understand, so before you know it, you're telling her about the fight you had with your boyfriend.

I sense your nerves as soon as I walk out to get you in the waiting room and I want more than anything just to give you a hug, to let you know I care. But I don't, because I know that would scare you and make you really uncomfortable. Instead, I use my smile and my words to let you know I care, and that you are important to me. I know you're still wary, so my goal for this session is just to build a bridge with you and invite you to share a bit of yourself with me. I know it will take time, but I am patient. To me, it's worth it. You are worth it.

I hear about your fight with your boyfriend and I sense the pain underneath your dismissive words as you say he's just being a jerk. I listen, not offering any words of advice, but I hear your pain. I hear inklings of your story as you tell me about the fight, and I sense that these themes of rejection and abandonment are part of your struggle. As I offer words of understanding and empathy, I sense you fighting back tears. Your face looks stoic and you say nothing, but I can hear you tell me about your sadness. Even without words, I hear you.

You don't know how she does it, but somehow this doctor is able to put into words how you feel. You feel a mass of pain inside you that's so big and unnameable that you don't know how to deal with it. You can't even put words to any of it and you can't tell anyone how you're feeling. Yet somehow she sees inside you, and something tight and hard inside you unravels just a tiny bit as you sense that she understands you. But still you hesitate. Is this for real? Is she for real? You put the wall back up, unsure if you can trust her. Is she just giving you a line, or does she really get you? You're going to keep coming, to see if she's for real.

THREE
Why Eleven to Fourteen?

On average, self-injury begins between the ages of eleven to fourteen. In *A Bright Red Scream*, Marilee Strong quotes Lisa Cross, who explains why girls of junior high age have a higher tendency to struggle with self-injury.

> Add in social and cultural pressures—which lead teenage girls to define their bodies by their attractiveness, while boys define theirs by strength and function—and it is easy to understand what a perilous passage puberty can be for young women. In fact, it is puberty that first introduces bleeding and body fat into a girl's life, two very powerful symbols of the loss of control over her body.[28]

Author Karen Conterio points out that there could be a strong connection between girls entering puberty and feelings of violation against their bodies, especially girls who have been sexually abused.

---

28 Strong, Marilee. *A Bright Red Scream: Self-Mutilation and the Language of Pain* (New York, NY: Viking, 1998), p. 125.

If someone feels powerless as a result of having been sexually violated, puberty can seem like another violation of the body... Some girls attempt to turn back the clock by starving themselves in order to return to their premenstrual child's body. Many cutters, even those who aren't anorexic, are discomfited by the sense of a loss of control over the body and its functions with the onset of menstruation and other physical changes at puberty.[29]

The feeling of being betrayed by one's own body can be even more traumatizing depending on the family situation. While personal identity is being formed and created during adolescence, family dynamics can play a huge role in how young people respond to the drastic internal and external changes brought on by the unset of puberty.

Since many cutters come from enmeshed families—where identity, family role, and boundary are confused—the task of establishing an independent identity is much more difficult. And if a girl has only a tenuous internal representation of herself to begin with, she may fear that the physical changes wrought by puberty will make her into someone else—a stranger unrecognizable to herself.[30]

Identity formation in junior high is unavoidable, but teaching young people who they are in Christ is also unavoidable. When we leave them to figure out who they are by themselves with no positive reinforcement from leaders, teachers, and parents, they're left to form personal identities centred only in how they see themselves physically, and what they hear on the playground and hallways of their schools. We need to start speaking to them in a way that communicates that they are children of God, that their talents go beyond their looks.

As a young person tries to gather who they are, what they're good at, and how they fit into this world, it is essential that we help

---

29 Ibid., p. 53.

30 Ibid., p. 54.

them establish what is "normal" during adolescent development. In a study in the Journal of Clinical Child Psychology, a group of researchers determined four factors contributing to high stress among adolescents. The most stressful factors were parental relationships and peer relationships.

Adolescents typically identified stressful situations involving school, family, and social contexts, whereas they infrequently depicted issues related to health and recreational activities. Subjects commonly identified issues concerning themselves or their parents and less frequently described stressful situations regarding a boyfriend/girlfriend, peer, or supervisor. Females' stressful episodes involving a boyfriend/girlfriend more often than did males. Females tended to employ Seeks Social Support and Wishful Thinking coping strategies, whereas males used more Avoidance. African-American children used more coping strategies than did Caucasian children and more frequently appraised a stressful episode as one that could be changed.[31]

> When I spoke those words, I heard in my heart a voice that said to me, "Daughter of mine. You are loved beyond your wildest dreams. Let me protect and save you." I said, "Alright," and broke down. Later that night, I told my whole youth group what I was doing and I received a whole group of support... They became my accountability partners. The unfortunate thing was that after I came home from this retreat, my parents convinced me I had been brainwashed and nothing would change. I believed them and I tried to commit suicide twice in the next two days.
> - Anonymous

What scares me about these findings is that the students chose wishful thinking and avoidance as two of their top three coping mechanisms. This means that no one is speaking positivity into their lives. No one is talking about their emotions, emotions which they are often feeling for the first time. If our adolescents are dealing with their stress with

---

31 Cornell Research Program on Self-Injurious Behaviour in Adolescents and Young Adults. "Coping Research." Date of Access: July 2012 (http://www.crpsib.com/userfiles/File/Annotated%20Bib%20Coping.pdf).

wishful thinking and avoidance, the deeper issues of self-injury won't be addressed. The behaviour will continue until they seek help.

Why do I say that the behaviour won't change?

During adolescent development, a young person's internal biological changes have a direct correlation on their behaviour. For instance, their internal changes will affect their outward appearance, which will in turn affect how they view themselves. This new self-image will change their outward behaviour. Also, those same behaviours will create a response from friends and family members—and those responses will change

> ...I didn't like it. Little did I know it would soon lead into being my way of coping. I began to cut in the August before I started Grade 8. I cut because I felt alone. I felt like I wasn't good enough for anyone, that no one cared. I felt like everyone was looking at me and thinking, *She's useless, let's keep moving.*
> - Erica

how their self-worth is formed. Such responses can range from mentioning body growth in both boys and girls to pointing out a boy's squeaky, cracking voice. Self-image and self-worth are so key to self-injury that it's no surprise that kids struggle through these types of hurt.

We need to make sure our youth groups are safe places for those who struggle with these issues. I received the following email in regards to how a self-injurer feels about their safety within their own group:

> If my church knew I cut, burned, scratched, or did anything of the sort, I would be removed from ministry so fast I wouldn't be able to blink. The one place I love and long to be involved in would be taken away, even with the best intentions, and I can't let that happen. Thus, I live a life of secrets. I help the youth as best I can but tell very little of where I've come from or why I don't date.[32]

Imagine if that person felt accepted and cared for enough to share their story. Imagine how many future lives they could speak into if they felt their life would not come crashing down around them once they were honest about their own struggles.

---

32 Anonymous Email

Within all our ministries will be someone who struggles with self-harm. We need to allow the process of healing to be one of acceptance and care, not one of judgment. Why are we not addressing these issues at home and in our churches? Are we afraid of the life-changing conversations that will need to happen afterward? Are we unwilling to walk through life with the very same kids that we were walking with before they told us about the self-injury in their lives?

Does our own security come before their insecurity? If it does, I'll give you the same line one of my professors gave me during my studies in the Arrow Leadership[33] program: "Suck it up, princess." That is my response, too. Instead of walking away from someone in need, suck up your pride, suck up your ego, and grow up. I say that to everyone, whether you're four, forty-four, or a hundred and four. It doesn't matter what age you are. We all need to grow up and look in the mirror in search of the caring human being God calls us to be in Matthew 22.

Speakers and researchers usually reference self-injurers with some sort of feminine noun, because it is statistically correct. I'm not saying that guys do not struggle, because I have talked with hundreds of guys who do. In fact, though there are fewer of them, guys usually harm themselves more severely than their female counterparts. Guys have been known to take their own lives without meaning to. Have you heard of anything more heart-breaking then someone taking his or her own life without actually trying

> I was living two lives. One was the perfect daughter, student, and Christian, though I use the word loosely. I knew about God, prayed the pray, went to church, served all the good things, but the other half of me was confused, scared, hurt, and dying. I couldn't live with both. They wouldn't go together, so I shut them down. Life become gray and I became a better actress.
> - Anonymous

to? Someone who was trying to cope with their emotions the only way they knew how and ended up having everything they had taken away by mistake?

Age doesn't matter, but it is on the rise. The number of parents who have come to me and admitted that they still struggle has been eye-opening. These are parents anywhere from forty to eighty years

---

33 Arrow Leadership. www.arrowleadership.org (accessed Jan. 2012).

old who are dealing with this issue. They come up to me after I finish talking and say something like, "I can't believe you just spoke on that, because I have been cutting in silence for over twenty years. Thank you."

I recently had the opportunity to speak at an event called Creation. While speaking on the main stage, I announced that I would be speaking during a breakout session later that day on self-injury; if anyone wanted to know more, they could come by. At least three people said to me after my main stage talk that no one would show up for a breakout on self-injury. Well, it's funny how things work out. Those three people were all in the front few rows when I spoke to the four to five thousand people who showed up that afternoon.

After the talk, I stayed to talk with those who had come. A couple walked up and told me they had been about to leave when the husband turned to his wife.

"Honey, I cut," he said.

She went on to tell me that she ripped into him, thinking he was joking and kidding around after my talk. But then she noticed the tears.

"Brett, I thought people who cut were Goth, wore black all the time, or they were people who wear long-sleeve shirts in the summer. Brett, I'm a fifty-year-old youth pastor. I wear Abercrombie and Fitch. I'll never look at self-injury in the same way again."

If you're over thirty, you might remember when this person came out publically about the role of self-injury in her life.

When no one listens to you, or you feel like no one is listening to you, all sorts of things start to happen. For instance, you have so much pain inside of yourself, you try to hurt yourself on the outside because you want help, but it is the wrong help you are asking for. People see it as crying wolf, or attention seeking, and they think because you are in the media all the time you've got enough attention. But I was actually crying out because I wanted to get better in order to go forward and continue my duty and role as wife, mother. So, yes, I did inflict upon myself. I didn't like myself. I was ashamed because I couldn't cope with the pressure.[34]

That was Princess Diana. The years were 1985–86, and this was one of the first times that self-injury actually came out in the media and people began to talk about it. These days, many other actors, singers, and performers share their stories with the media in order to hopefully help someone who might be in the very same situation they found themselves in.

Angelina Jolie told *Rolling Stone* about her life of self-injury and how it was the investment in time and the little things in life that would trigger her emotions.

"I didn't really want to live," she says, "so anything that was an investment in time made me angry... but also I just felt sad." When the hopelessness is hurting you, it's the fixtures and fittings that finish you off. "I sat on the floor and cried, because I was trying to pick out carpet color and I thought that I wasn't going to live to put it in," she remembers. "I couldn't sleep. I always felt like I wanted to burn harder or go faster than everything around me, always. I lived very very much inside. Now I actually share my life with somebody who burns harder than I do and sleeps less than I do and needs to live fiercely and matches me. He calms me, because I never feel crazy around him, and I always felt crazy.[35]

34 BBC. "The Panorama Interview." Date of Access: March 2012 (http://www.bbc.co.uk/news/special/politics97/diana/panorama.html).

35 Rolling Stone. "Blood Sugar Sex Magic." Date of Access: February 2012 (http://

Jolie, in the same interview, spoke about her battle with cutting and how she felt when she couldn't find the help she needed. She relied on her boyfriend at the time for the help she needed, who was unable to provide it.

> Looking back, I think I was probably not good for him. He was somebody that I wanted to help me break out and I would get frustrated when he couldn't help me. Which was when the knives came in—he'd be asked to cut me or I'd cut him.[36]

Others keep coming forward to tell their stories of anorexia, bulimia, binge eating, depression, and even battles with suicide. Megan Fox opened up in an article from *Rolling Stone* about her battle with self-loathing and how that affected her life.

> I'm really insecure about everything. I never think I'm worthy of anything… I have a sick feeling of being mocked all the time. I have a lot of self-loathing. Self-loathing doesn't keep me from being happy. But that doesn't mean I don't struggle. I am very vulnerable. But I can be aggressive, hurtful, domineering and selfish, too. I'm emotionally unpredictable and all over the place. I'm a control freak…
>
> But I don't want to elaborate. I would never call myself a cutter. Girls go through different phases when they're growing up, when they're miserable and do different things, whether it's an eating disorder or they dabble in cutting.[37]

We'll continue to look at some of those stories in the sections ahead, because we can draw inspiration, words of wisdom, and hope from hearing

---

www.rollingstone.com/news/story/5938014/blood_sugar_sex_magic).
36 Ibid.

37 E!Online. "Megan Fox Talks Cutting, Stabbing & Eating Disorders." Date of Access: July 2012 (http://ca.eonline.com/news/144459/megan-fox-talks-cutting-stabbing-eating-disorders).

the stories of other people who have struggled, who are struggling, and those who have been able to get the help they needed to move on.

Johnny Depp, in an interview, talked about how any scar, whether from a tattoo artist or a knife, tell a story.

My body is like a journal in a way… It's like what sailors used to do, where very tattoo meant something, a specific time in your life where you mark on yourself, whether you do it to yourself with a knife or with a professional tattoo artist.[38]

As we continue to share our stories, we can become a beacon of light for someone close to us. In his memoir, *My Booky Wook*, Russell Brand explained the effect cutting has on him.

I get fixated when I am bleeding—I can see why they went for bloodletting in medieval times because it makes you feel a bit better. When I cut myself, the drama of it kind of calms me down. It doesn't usually have that effect on other people, though.[39]

I think it's important to note that even he realizes that the calming effect is not the reaction that should come from harming yourself. A scar that was once defined by a life of turmoil can be a story of hope for someone just beginning his or her battle with self-injury.

Self-harm also isn't about seeking attention. I love what L.R. Pembroke wrote:

If it was attention I was after I would take my clothes off and walk into the street.[40]

38 Strong, Marilee. *A Bright Red Scream: Self-Mutilation and the Language of Pain.* (New York, NY: Viking, 1998), p. 138.

39 Brand, Russell. *My Booky Wook: A Memoir of Sex, Drugs, and Stand-Up.* (New York, NY: Collins, 2009), p. 171.

40 The National Self-Harm Network. "Self-Injury: Myths and Common Sense." Date of Access: August 8, 2012 (http://www.kreativeinterventions.com/Pembroke&Smith1.pdf).

Other students had written to me and said things like, "My main goal in self-injury is to feel something, to feel anything."

Another question I am asked regularly is this: "Brett, I have a friend who cuts, but they have only cut twice. Does that make them a self-injurer?"

There is no statistic that tells you if you're a self-injurer, or not. There's no fan sticker that you receive if you cut more than five times, and there's no limit to what makes you a self-injurer. Here are the questions you do need to ask:

1. Do you hurt yourself? Do you deliberately cause physical harm to yourself to the extent of causing tissue damage?
2. Why? What is the reason you are doing this?

This includes bruising, bleeding, and anything else that causes tissue damage. Do you cause this harm to yourself to deal with unpleasant or overwhelming emotions, thoughts, or situations? If you answered yes to the first question, I hope you would take the time to seek help from someone you trust and then seek help from a doctor or counsellor. It doesn't matter if you hurt yourself once, twice, or over twenty times, because self-injury is a cycle.

IN THE THERAPIST'S OFFICE
Session Three: by Dr. Merry Lin

TODAY, YOU'RE FEELING MORE RELAXED ABOUT COMING AND YOU ACTUALLY kind of look forward to seeing your shrink. Last session was pretty fun, just looking at magazines and stuff, but you have no idea what kind of therapy would ever let you just look at pictures. What's also weird is that she hasn't even brought up the whole cutting thing, even though that's what made your parents freak out and bring you to see her. But whatever.

The shrink comes out of her office and gives you a huge grin. She's always smiling and laughing, so you don't mind hanging out with her. You know she's probably old and all that, but somehow she's fun to be with and you feel like she can relate to you. Like she somehow gets you and really likes being with you. She isn't at all what you expected from a doctor. It's kind of weird to call a shrink by her first name, but she keeps insisting that you do it, so okay, if that's what she wants, you oblige.

I see that you're more relaxed and that's great to see. My goal for today is to continue building a bridge with you so that you can begin to trust me. I can see the real you beneath the walls you put up, and I'm just aching to help you see how awesome you really are. I know you have a story to tell me and I'm really looking forward to hearing it bit by bit. I know that somehow the heartache and pain you've experienced has caused you to doubt yourself and to wonder if anyone could ever really get you or see you as worthy of love, but that's how I see you. You are beautiful both inside and out. Oh, I cannot wait until you see yourself that way! It's what keeps me doing this; what an amazing front row seat I get to see as God's tender love unearths the treasure he has created in you, something the world keeps tearing down day by day. But I'm ready to fight for the truth of your value, because you are so worth it.

You walk into the shrink's office and see your collage from last week sitting on the table. Hey, it's actually pretty creative with all the pictures and words you cut out. You especially like the way you used colour and fonts to look kind of edgy and cool. As you sit down, you find yourself chatting with her about your week. Nothing really important, but you're feeling more and more comfortable with her. After a while, she asks you to tell her about each part of your collage, just something that attracted you to cutting out each picture or word. As you ramble on, she listens and nods, saying a few things that encourage you to keep talking.

She then asks you about some of the themes she sees in your collage. She points out the pictures of all these great-looking and happy couples hugging, interspersed with pictures of girls on their own looking sad and lonely, with the word "EMO" in huge letters slashed across their pictures. There's also this really great picture you found of a castle with a huge stonewall and moat around the entire thing and the word "trapped" going sideways around the wall. She notices that there's a picture of some teens standing around laughing and looking really cool, right next to the words "Tragically Hip." She talks about the other words you cut out, like "loser" and "freak" and "stupid" and "love 4ever," and she asks if part of your story includes this theme of rejection and isolation and the message that somehow you don't fit in. And yet maybe there's also a secret longing to belong and for someone to just love you.

Boy, she really gets you. Who knew that a bunch of magazine pictures could tell her so much of what's going on inside you? You look at your collage more closely and start to feel a real sadness as you hear her tell you what she sees, but at the same time you feel warmth, since she understands you and your story in a way you didn't even know. She's so good at putting into words what you can't even express or understand about what's going on inside. You feel just a little bit less alone. And also just a little bit less awkward and weird, because she seems to really like all the odd things about you that have always made you feel different from everyone else.

You also like that she seems to listen to you rather than always talking at you, like most grown-ups do. Just because you're quiet doesn't mean you don't have things to say. You're starting to think that you want to keep coming.

FOUR
The Self-Injury Cycle

We begin with negative emotions. When a negative situation arises in your life, you have a corresponding emotional response—and that response creates tension. For some, this leads to a disassociation from the reality of what they know they should do. They lead themselves away from the known response to the unknown release of self-injury. Before the act of self-injury, their thoughts tell them, *No one likes me. I can't stand my life. I'm so stupid. My life just sucks.* During self-injury, their thoughts tell them, *I need to hurt myself. This is the only way. I have to do this.*

The cycle then continues, because there are positive effects. You feel alive; the endorphin release feels really good. But the problem is that once those effects wear off, the negative effects stroll in—thoughts like, *I can't believe I just hurt myself. I can't tell anyone about this. When am I going to stop doing this?*

Those negative emotions then lead right back into negative effects, which leads to tension, which takes us back to disassociation from reality, to self-injury, to negative effects… The cycle continues over and over again. You might not self-injure again the same day, or even the same month, but the cycle will continue to spiral until you take a stand.

A girl who has written to me a couple of times noticed this cycle in her own life. She wrote:

> I don't understand why when I hurt myself I feel happy and relieved, but I do. Unfortunately the feeling does not last and after the feeling of happiness comes guilt, sorrow and more pain.

The positive effects come in like a small river, but the negative effects of self-injury come in like a tsunami.

PEOPLE STOP SELF-INJURING

In the first few months after making the decision to read every book I could find on self-injury, I was depressed to read about the effects, causes, and stories of the individuals who suffered. One night, I opened a book and found the following words inscribed on the inside cover: "There is hope, there is solutions." I went to bed feeling hopeful. If you find yourself feeling like the darkness and loneliness is taking a hold on your life, take these words from C.S. Lewis and imprint them in your heart:

The bad dream will be over: it will be morning.[41]

In *Bodily Harm*, the authors say, "Is giving up your coping strategy and facing your fears worth it? Because only you can say for sure."[42] Why should you, or your friends, stop? That's our question, because we're only looking at this from three perspectives. Either we self-injure,

> I felt like since I couldn't speak up or stand up for myself, I decided to take my pain out on myself as a way to release how I was feeling. I would remember locking myself in the school bathroom and slicing my back and arms with scissors and any other blunt object. I hated what I was doing to myself, but I refused to stop.
> - Anonymous

---

41 Lewis, C S. *Mere Christianity: A Revised and Amplified Edition, with a New Introduction, of the Three Books, Broadcast Talks, Christian Behaviour, and Beyond Personality.* (San Francisco, CA: HarperSanFrancisco, 2001), p. 170.

42 Conterio, Karen, Wendy Lader, and Jennifer K. Bloom. *Bodily Harm: The Breakthrough Treatment Program for Self-Injurers.* (New York, NY: Hyperion, 1998), p. 227.

we have friends who self-injure now, or we will know friends who self-injure in the future. This could be before you graduate, before marriage, or even before next summer; we never know when someone will disclose to us that they struggle with self-injury. We have to be ready to have this discussion at any time.

> My parents would relentlessly interrogate me, asking all kinds of questions I couldn't answer. If I did answer, they weren't satisfied. They just kept at it and at it, making things worse. And in my mind, giving me more reason and more motivation to cut: to cut deeper, to draw more blood, or to eat less. You name it, I had it in my head that I was worthless and that no one loved or cared about me.
> - Anonymous

The first reason to stop is that self-injury just doesn't seem to work. It doesn't release the tension like it did at the beginning. Like with alcohol resistance, the body defends against that quick endorphin release. Self-injury, therefore, becomes less effective over time.

The second reason is that we desire to be healthier. Whether it's mentally, physically, spiritually, or emotionally, we can stop self-injuring and look towards a better future.

The third reason may not be the best, or the most effective, but we might stop self-injuring in response to pressure from someone we love. Unfortunately, we can only stop if *we want to stop*. I have found the following quote extremely powerful:

> …They are more than their disorder, their lives infinitely richer, their stories more complex, than a single label might indicate.[43]

I cannot stand labels. Self-injury is a struggle, but it can be overcome. It is a season in life, and seasons do change.

I have heard people say, "My scars are a reminder of all the times I needed help and did not get it." In my research, I read an interesting novel called *Cut*, in which a young girl, Callie, struggles with cutting.

---

43 Strong, Marilee. *A Bright Red Scream: Self-Mutilation and the Language of Pain*. (New York, NY: Viking, 1998), p. xv.

At one point, she has a conversation with her counsellor about it. When Callie tries to hand over all the objects she could use to cut herself, her counsellor replies,

> There are all kinds of things in the world you could use to hurt yourself. All kinds of things you could turn into weapons. Even if you wanted to give them all to me, it would be impossible… I can't keep you safe, only you can."[44]

If you're reading this today and you are like Callie, realize that you're the only person who can stop. No pastor, teacher, or counsellor can tell you to stop; the decision has to come from you, when you come to a place where you can say, "This doesn't work."

Out of the over ten thousand emails I've received from those who self-injure, not one of them ever says it's an easy way to cope. Instead, they say it's the only way they know how to cope.

Where do we come in, as friends who want to help someone we know? Karen Conterio says:

> …but screaming out silently with no way to express what was going on in my life—that's where God found me. He put a street help organization in my life to show me I could be loved. They weren't disgusted by me
> - Anonymous

> There is nobody on earth who can, or will, save you from yourself. You are going to have to do it for yourself—but not by yourself.[45]

That last little pause, "but not by yourself," is where we come in as friends. We need to walk alongside those who self-injure and do whatever is asked of us in order to help the healing process. That means, however, that we can't be the ones to make you stop. 1 Thessalonians

---

44 McCormick, Patricia. *Cut* (Asherville, NC: Front Street, 2000), p. 126.

45 Conterio, Karen, Wendy Lader, and Jennifer Kingson Bloom. *Bodily Harm: The Breakthrough Treatment Program for Self-Injurers* (New York, NY: Hyperion, 1998), p. x.

paints a great picture of the support structure and hope we can give to those we know who self-injure.

> So let's not sleepwalk through life like those others. Let's keep our eyes open and be smart. People sleep at night and get drunk at night. But not us! Since we're creatures of Day, let's act like it. Walk out into the daylight sober, dressed up in faith, love, and the hope of salvation.
> God didn't set us up for an angry rejection but for salvation by our Master, Jesus Christ. He died for us, a death that triggered life. Whether we're awake with the living or asleep with the dead, we're alive with him! So speak encouraging words to one another. Build up hope so you'll all be together in this, no one left out, no one left behind. I know you're already doing this; just keep on doing it.
> (1 Thessalonians 5:6–11)

Stopping has to be a conscious decision. It won't be easy, but it comes down to where you see hope coming from and who can speak hope into your life. It's sad how many of us are great friends when the times are fantastic but bail when the tough realities of life set in. We run away and hide from the dirtiness of true friendship.

Philippians 2 starts off with a challenge for us to be deep-spirited friends with one another. Such friendship is required from those of us are helping someone through this season of their life.

> If you've gotten anything at all out of following Christ, if his love has made any difference in your life, if being in a community of the Spirit means anything to you, if you have a heart, if you care—then do me a favor: Agree with each other, love each other, be deep-spirited friends. Don't push your way to the front; don't sweet-talk your way to the top. Put yourself aside, and help others get ahead. Don't be obsessed with getting your own advantage. Forget yourselves long enough to lend a helping hand.
> (Philippians 2:1–4)

Do you think your friend's pain will get better from you running away from the situation? No. Running away only adds to their pain. The problem is that we struggle with speaking hope and encouragement into the lives of our friends who deal with self-injury.

Cutting affects so much more than a gender, ethnicity, or cultural subgroup. I've been approached thousands of times for people to disclose to me—for the first time to anyone—that they self-injure. They admit to themselves that they no longer want to live that way and no longer want to live in silence.

So many people hurt in silence and struggle with self-harm every day. However, there are healthy ways to cope with emotional distress. Earlier we talked about hiding the objects that cause the self-harm, just like in the Foo Fighters song. We also mentioned that some people cope through holding ice when they feel the urge to cut, an act which releases endorphins.

Another coping technique uses imagery to divert a person's attention away from acts of self-injury.

> Imagery can be used in two ways. First, it can be used to divert your attention. To use imagery to do this, you create an imaginary situation which you find pleasant. Make your imaginary setting as specific and detailed as you possibly can.
>
> The second way of using imagery is more specific. "In this technique, you first identify the area in your body where you feel tension. Once you have found that place, you then try to imagine and describe what the tension looks like." And once you have described the physical sensation as fully as possible, it can be changed. This use of imagery can change your physical sensations. "Using imagery makes it possible to relieve stress and tension and enhance relaxation."[46]

---

46 Self-Injury.net. "Distractions." Date of Access: August 8, 2012 (http://self-injury.net/ information-recovery/recovery/distractions). Quoted material taken from *Scarred Souls*, by Tracy Alderman.

When we visualize the tension areas in our body and describe the feeling, we begin to verbalize everything that we feel, allowing us to become more comfortable talking about our feelings. We also have time to verbalize the connection between the tension and how it relates to the emotions running through our bodies. When I'm away speaking, a few people in every crowd will come up and acknowledge that they either cut or hurt themselves in other ways. These same people have their own ways of coping, and many of them are on their own journeys to restore their bodies and leave self-injury behind.

> Tomorrow I will look in the mirror and find another piece of who I really am. I will get that much closer to becoming someone I love again. I will get that much closer to stop hating myself, but I am still depressed and still a little negative. I'm working on it one step at a time. If I can do it,
> so can you.
> - Zoey

As I've already said, I hate labels. If you deal with cutting, note that you are not a "cutter." It is your struggle. You can get beyond it. It is not your identity. It is not who you are. It is not the only thing you are about. Your identity is found in Christ, because we are his workmanship.

For we are his workmanship, created in Christ Jesus for good works, which God prepared beforehand, that we should walk in them. (Ephesians 2:10, ESV)

Identity is not found in cutting, but in Christ who created us not to suffer but to do his work. He paid our way out of pain and suffering, so we can choose whether or not we want our identity to be rooted in self-injury, or in him. This is only part of the healing process, however. If you're not a believer, the will be to find your identity in something other than your self-injury. You need to realize that you are not your disorder.

IN THE THERAPIST'S OFFICE
Session Four: by Dr. Merry Lin

YOU'RE IN THE WAITING ROOM, FURIOUS AT YOUR PARENTS FOR MAKING YOU come today, so mad that you can hardly sit still. Of all days, today was *not* the day you wanted to spend time talking about your stupid feelings. It was a completely horrible and brutal week; you just broke up with your total jerk of a boyfriend. You feel so stressed and uptight that it takes everything in you not to scream. You think it's nobody's business, and besides, no one really cares anyway, so you do everything you can to keep your feelings inside. Your parents don't even know that you're upset. They'd just freak out and give you a big, long lecture… just what you don't need.

This week, you really let yourself have it. You couldn't seem to stop the slashing. It's the only way you could get through, but even as you think about it, you go into numb mode. You just shut it all down.

Whatever.

Who cares?

I come out of the office to get you. Before you even notice me, I see your pain. I can tell it's been a bad week for you. I see that you've worn your long sleeve sweatshirt, even though it's a hot day. You follow me into my office, but the look on your face tells me that you don't want to talk at all. You slump into the same chair, cross your arms, and look away from me, refusing to look me in the eye. I can tell that you're seething with anger and that everything in you doesn't want to be here. You're doing everything possible to push me away, but it's not going to work. I'm not put off by your anger and my back doesn't go up at all. Instead, I push into your anger to pursue you because I know that underneath your protective shell of anger is a world of hurt.

I speak softly and ask if it's been a bad week. You snort, thinking how brilliant this doctor is with her PhD and everything that she's able to state the obvious.

No kidding, lady.

However, deep down, something in you wants to tell her everything that has happened. You fight it, because you still don't know if you can really trust her. But you decide to test her: if you tell her about all the cutting, maybe she'll get mad at you and lock you up in the loony bin. So you tell the shrink straight up that you've been cutting all week. Like, every day. You wait for her to respond, keeping your eyes down, heart beating fast. You pretend like you don't care, but on the inside you're afraid of what she's going to say. Is she going to lecture you on all the evils of cutting?

Is she going to start praying loudly over you and casting out demons or something?

Is she going to tell your parents?

You're sure her view of you is going to change somehow, and everything after that is going to tank for sure.

I see the internal wrestling going on in you. When you finally tell me that you've been cutting all week, my heart breaks for you. I know that you've had a really tough week and that you're coping in the only way you know how. I can tell that you're really hurting and I want more than anything for you to know that I'm here for you and that I care. I know that it's hard for you to trust me and that you're just waiting for the other shoe to drop. So, I understand the walls you put up to protect yourself, but I'm patient and I will wait for you. I will not give up on you.

When you finally look up and peek quickly at her face, you see her warm eyes. You can tell she's not angry or upset at you. You don't know how she does it, but somehow you feel safe with her. It's like you know she isn't going to judge you. Before you know it, you find yourself telling her about the breakup with your boyfriend. She listens carefully and says things here and there that show you that she understands you. You don't know how she does, it but you just keep talking and talking. As you open up, you feel the knot in your stomach finally release. Soon, you find yourself crying, something you *never* do in front of anyone else. But somehow you feel that it's okay to show her a bit of what's going on in your inside world with her.

She ends the session by teaching you how to do some deep breathing to help you relax.

Go figure.

You think you knew how to breathe, but it turns out that you don't breathe deep enough most of the time. After doing the deep breathing with her, you feel super relaxed in a way that you haven't felt in a long time. In the end, you think that maybe it was a good thing you came for your session.

FIVE
Suicide

I hate when the phone rings first thing in the morning, especially before breakfast. I get a chill every time it happens. I get a chill because of the conversation I know is often about to happen. It's usually a principal calling to book me to speak at a school. When I ask when they want me to come in, this is what I hear: "Today, if you're available. We had a student commit suicide last night and would like you to come talk to our students. We really do not know what to do."

First off, what kind of world are we living in when we have Grade Four students who don't want to be a part of it any longer? My response to the principal is always the same: "No, I can't."

I'm not a crisis team, I'm not a counsellor, and this book won't have all the answers. What I do as a speaker is come to your schools before tragedy strikes. If I come after a tragedy, all I can do is help bandage the wounds and feelings that are left over. In reality, no speaker in the world can walk in and make things okay... because things are not okay. If you're reading this book and are thinking about suicide, or if you struggle with self-injury, please contact a counsellor, your youth leader, or talk to your parents.

Two months after I spoke at an elementary school last year, a seventh-grader there took her own life. To anyone in my audiences or reading this book, my advice can be summed up in two words: Hold on!

No matter what you're going through, hold on.

No matter how tough your situation is, hold on.

No matter how much you want your pain to be over, hold on.

What you're going through is not representative of your entire life; it's only a season, and seasons change. Bruce Cockburn sings that we need to "kick at the darkness till it bleeds daylight."[47]

I cannot guarantee things will get better today, tomorrow, next month, or even next year. But it will, and I want you to be around to see the season of your life change.

If you're thinking of suicide, please talk to a counsellor.

Suicide rates have been on a great incline over the last forty years, but the findings from The Jed Foundation are troubling, to say the least.

This is a dramatic and huge increase," Hayes said. "We need to look at the spike and we need to ask questions about it."

Between 1990 and 2003 the suicide rate for 10- to 24-year-olds decreased 28.5 percent, from 9.48 to 6.78 of 100,000 persons. A downward trend, however, was reversed in 2003, with an 8-percent spike in the same age group.

The largest increases were attributed to females. Among 10- to 14-year-old females, a 75.9-percent jump was recorded. Rates for females ages 15 to 19 years rose by 32.3 percent from 265 to 355 persons and rates for males ages 15 to 19 increased by 9 percent, from 1,222 to 1,345 out of every 100,000 persons.[48]

Suicide is the act of taking your own life. Let's talk about the myths and realities of suicide.

---

47 Cockburn, Bruce. "Lovers in a Dangerous Time." New York, NY: Columbia, 1984.

48 The Jed Foundation. "Suicide Rates See Largest Spike in Past 10 Years." Date of Access: July 2012 (http://www.jedfoundation.org/press-room/news-archive/suicide-rates-see-largest-spike-in-past-10-years).

Only crazy people think about suicide. All kinds of people have suicidal thoughts. There's not just one type of person who struggles with this. Yet so many people think that they're crazy because they have suicidal thoughts. We have to stop putting labels and stigmas on self-injury, because they cause additional confusion for people already coping with confusing thoughts and feelings.

Young people rarely think about suicide. Teens and suicide are more closely linked than any adult would like to admit. One particular story has stuck with me over the years. A girl told me, "I think I know why I cut and why I'm anorexic."

"Why?"

"Well, last year my mom left my dad."

I responded, "I am so sorry."

"That was not it," she said. "I came home and found my dad hanging in the garage."

"Honey, that is definitely why you struggle."

I've heard dozens of variations on this story. I don't know if I would be the same man I am today if I had found my dad's body when I was in Grade Eight.

In an article entitled "40% of Kids Who Attempt Suicide First Try in Elementary or Middle School," *Time Magazine* posted some scary statistics when it came to junior high kids and suicide. The study found that suicide rates increased greatly once a child turned twelve.

> Researchers at the University of Washington surveyed 883 young adults ages 18 or 19 about previous suicide attempts and learned that 78—close to 9%—had tried to commit suicide.[49]

The fact is that young people, even as young as nine, are starting to struggle with suicidal thoughts. We need to have tough conversations

---

49 *Time Magazine.* "40% of Kids Who Attempt Suicide First Try in Elementary or Middle School. Date of Access: January 2012 (http://healthland.time.com/2011/11/30/ study-40-of-kids-who-attempt-suicide-first-try-in-elementary-or-middle-school/#ixzz1lFUsh5gh).

with our kids, conversations that scare us as parents. In the long run, though, it will be well worth it.

Talking about suicide gives people permission to do it. Years ago, the television show *Boston Public* aired an episode about a suicide club. I remember thinking it was a little crazy, but then I really began to think about it. The reality is talking about suicide actually dissuades people from going through with it. Counsellors have told me that one of the largest factors in a person not taking their life is realistically talking about it. A person's willingness to listen to someone and converse is encouraging. By talking about suicide and self-injury, are we not teaching our kids how to properly deal with all the new emotional responses that come with adolescence?

> As kids, by and large, self injurers were not allowed to have or express their own feelings—especially anger. Instead they were forced to carry the feelings of their parents and grew up feeling responsible for their parents' anger, frustration and unhappiness…When a child's feelings and perceptions are actively denied or minimized by her parents, the child's ability to develop a language of feelings is stunted, and she is left with a mute hopelessness about the possibility of communicating in a way that will help her get critical needs met.[50]

I would rather talk to my kids about their feelings and find out that they're struggling emotionally than find out too late and realize that as a parent I didn't give them the emotional support they needed—all because I thought that if we talked about it, it could become a reality.

Suicide is sudden and unpredictable. The most common response from people who've had to deal with a suicide in their lives is this one: "I had no clue." We usually find out a couple of months later that those same people change their response to, "I should have known." As much as we hate to admit it, suicide is unpredictable. It's a process, not a singular event or thought. I've found that there are usually eight to ten different

50 Strong, Marilee. *A Bright Red Scream: Self-Mutilation and the Language of Pain.* (New York, NY: Viking, 1998) p. 44.

ideas, or hints, that people will express before the attempt occurs. There are warning signs if you know what to look for.

Suicide is only a cry for attention. A friend of someone who committed suicide once explained why learning the deceit of this stereotype can so devastating. She hadn't been sleeping through the night while in high school and spent some nights in an online chat room. One night, while talking to one of her best friends, her friend brought up the fact that she was going to kill herself that night. The girl wrote "LOL," thinking that her best friend was joking around, only to find out that her best friend did, indeed, take her own life that night. This girl went on to tell me that every day she wishes she had done something about it, that she took her friend's words more seriously.

So what if we think someone is only seeking attention? This is life and death we're talking about. This is *life.* The attention we give them and the subsequent conversation we have might just save their life. So who cares what we think about their intentions? What matters is how they deal with their feelings. What matters is that *they might choose to live.*

Nothing can stop people from committing suicide. Just because a person has suicidal thoughts doesn't mean they want to die.

Let's return, for a moment, to the self-injury cycle. You start with some negative emotions surrounding an event in your life which produce negative effects. This leads right back into tension, which leads back to disassociation with reality, to self-injury, to negative effects. From here, the cycle continues over and over again.

There is a sense that suicide will stop the pain. The disassociation with reality is the fact that a successful suicide as a way to release pain is, in fact, death. The reality to suicide is death, but to the individual it is a solution to pain that overlooks death. If your ability to cope is stretched to the limit, or if problems occur together one after another, it death can seem like the only way to make this pain stop. People may see suicide as a way to stop pain. Their goal is to stop pain, not life.

Suicidal people will always be at risk. The reality is that there are probably very few people reading this book who have not thought, at one time or another, *I just want it to be over.*

For most of us, myself included, this goes away the moment it comes into our minds. The thought doesn't linger. However, for some of us the thoughts do linger, and they become a viable solution to the pain around us.

Statistically speaking, suicide is the second leading cause of death among the people between the ages of ten and twenty-four.[51]

On average, almost 3000 people commit suicide every day. Every 30 seconds, the loss of a person who killed themselves shatters the lives of family and friends. For every person who completes a suicide, 20 or more may attempt suicide.[52]

To put that into perspective, when I'm speaking and get to these statistics, which happens at the twenty-five minute marker, about fifty people have committed suicide somewhere.

Many of us kick ourselves when we make a mistake, feel angry, or upset about something and we assume that over time eventually these emotions will heal and dissipate, so we can move on with our lives. We learn ways to cope with struggles and overcome these negative feelings.[53]

Don't ever think that the only people who self-injure are those who cut. Cutting is the new anorexia, the new thing we seem to talk about. Anorexia and bulimia are still huge issues, especially when it comes to self-image, just as depression and suicide are still issues as well. Just because something is new doesn't elevate its importance, or take

51 The Jed Foundation. "Suicide Rates See Largest Spike in Past 10 Years." Date of Access: July 2012 (http://www.jedfoundation.org/press-room/news-archive/suicide-rates-see-largest-spike-in-past-10-years).

52 World Health Organization. "World Suicide Prevention Day." Date of Access: July 2012 (http://www.who.int/mediacentre/news/statements/2007/s16/en/index.html).

53 WashingtonParent.com. "A Cry For Help: What Parents of Teens Need to Know About Cutting." Date of Access: January 2012 (http://washingtonparent.com/articles/0502/cutting.html)

precedence from other issues. It just means that we need to learn about the issue. We still need to be careful not to dismiss or stop talking about other areas of self-injury.

For instance, some of us drink too much. Many experiment with drugs. A lot of people eat too much, going through cycles of binge eating and dieting. When I was in university, I would work out six to seven days a week for two hours a day. I was going through my own form of self-injury. I was breaking down my body. My tendons, bones, muscles, and ligaments were disintegrating. Too much of anything, including exercise, can constitute self-injury.

Other people gamble or have promiscuous sex. Actions are the things we do. Our actions can be forms of self-injury, and I would include promiscuous sex as self-injury. Erwin McManus, the pastor of Mosaic, a church in Los Angeles, says, "Fake intimacy is better than wide open loneliness." I know a lot of teens and young adults who just fall into bed with someone thinking they'll find some great closeness or compassion, but all they find is pain, guilt, and more sorrow. But our actions arise from our feelings.

The actions of self-injury, in their most general form, are outpourings of deeper issues. They are the wounding embraces of our lives, the hugs that hurt. No one just wakes up one morning and, while yawning through his or her morning stretch, decides to kill themselves that day. Nobody just wakes up and thinks, *Today I think I'll try a little meth.* Rather, we get up in the morning and we feel okay. But as the day passes, life punches us in the face. Maybe you get into a fight with your mom, or break up with your boyfriend or girlfriend. Perhaps you fail a test or get fired from your job. Maybe you're going through a divorce, have just endured the death of a loved one, or got a rejection letter in the mail.

Whatever your personal tragedy, the fact is that sometimes life has a hidden punch just waiting for us. That's when we go through a moment of not being able to take it anymore. That's when we feel a sense of abandonment. The single largest feeling in our teens and young adults generation is abandonment—not love, not compassion, not joy. Abandonment.

I hear about the word abandonment almost daily. I also hear the words "I'm drowning." I hear people say, "If one more thing happens, I'm going under." How do we reach in, grab that person's hand, and pull them up when they're going under?

IN THE THERAPIST'S OFFICE
Session Five: by Dr. Merry Lin

YOU'RE FEELING KIND OF FLAT AFTER HAVING SUCH A HORRIBLE WEEK LAST week. This has been a "good," week in that you haven't cut, but you're still feeling kind of sad and mad because you miss your boyfriend. You wonder if you have made a mistake, but no, you know it was the right thing to do, as you caught the idiot cheating with another girl.

What a total loser!

But now you're wondering if you're the loser for not seeing him for the complete nut job he was. How could you have missed that?

You've been practicing the deep breathing your shrink told you to do. To your surprise, it has helped you calm down when you're upset. You wonder what else she's going to teach you. At this point, you're starting to think that it's worth trying some different things, as you're tired of the same old, same old. You're also starting to believe that maybe you *do* have something to offer and that maybe there will be people out there who will get you and accept you the way you are.

You wonder what she has up her sleeve when you walk into her office and see on her table some ice cubes in a bowl, a rubber band, a teddy bear, a small treasure box, and some bubbles.

What the heck?

She greets you with a twinkle in her eye and laughs as she sees the face you make when you see the random things on the table.

Okay, this is getting weirder and weirder. You are, however, intrigued—in spite of yourself.

I love seeing your face when you see my "toys," but I especially love your willing attitude to trust your wonky therapist. You're such a delight and a joy to work with! Today, I want to introduce to you different ways of coping when you feel really stressed, anxious, upset, or emotional. I know that it's really hard for you to give up cutting as your way of coping if you don't have anything better to take its place. I also want you to have tools you can take home with you so that you can develop confidence in your own ability to cope, regardless of who might be around you to help you. I begin by talking about the cycle of pain, emotional turmoil, cutting, and what happens inside the brain, teaching you about the hormones that are released when you cut. I talk to you about ways to interrupt that cycle and fool the brain into accepting new ways of coping and responding to pain.

As you listen to your shrink, what she says makes a lot of sense. She talks about it in such a non-judgemental way that you don't feel like such a loser. You realize that there's a physiological reason that makes it even harder to just quit the cutting. As you hear her share the statistics on the number of teens who cut, you feel less alone and not quite so *emo*. Your gaze keeps going to the toys on her table and she notices, laughing again. She tells you about doing things that trigger your senses and make you feel something as a way of interrupting the self-injury cycle—something called "grounding," whatever that means. She puts the cold ice cubes in your hand; you shriek and almost drop them. But the cold ice against your skin definitely makes you feel pain. She tells you to try this the next time you're tempted to cut. Or you could jump into the shower and take a really cold shower.

Huh, who would have thought?

I love your teachable heart and how enthusiastically you respond to my ideas. I take the rubber band next and put it on your wrist, instructing you to try snapping it against your wrist. You wince as you try it and I tell you that it's an easy way to ground yourself, especially if you don't have ice or a cold shower nearby!

Then I switch gears and talk about ways to soothe yourself when you feel really crappy—from stroking and hugging a soft teddy bear; to taking a warm bubble bath; to imagining all your bad feelings and thoughts going into the treasure box, being locked up and then given to Jesus to take care of until you're ready to deal with them; to blowing bubbles, imagining your worries and fears going up into the sky and disappearing. I talk about how these different strategies help you refocus and distract yourself in positive ways. And of course, I remind you to do deep breathing every day, especially when you're feeling anxious or uptight.

Wow, you never knew there were so many other things you could try when you're upset or tense or numb. You promise that you're going to give some of these a try during the week and report back. You leave the session with a smile on your face, feeling a sense of hope that maybe things *could* be different in your life.

SIX
Abandonment

W hat do you feel abandoned from?

Our feelings come from somewhere deep within us. They come from our stories, our histories, and we all have them. Some feelings are easy to deal with. Maybe we didn't make the basketball team or we got fired… we can deal with those stories. But there are some things we are just not able to handle.

As a side note, when I talk about drugs and alcohol, I'm not necessarily talking about addiction. I'm talking about people who do these things to get beyond something in their lives. I once heard an Erwin McManus quote that goes like this:

Many of us, instead of facing the issues and dealing with them, are leading medicated lives because we do not have the strength to face the lives we already have.

Every once in a while, we have a really bad idea. And let's be honest—six beers works. I'm not saying it's okay to go and drink six beers if you have a bad day; I'm saying that when drugs and alcohol are used that way, they provide an escape from something we see no end to.

I've often heard that we cannot change what we will not acknowledge, so let's acknowledge what self-injury really is and how it affects our lives.

We know there's hope on the outside. People say they live in this dark hole in their head and they just don't know how to get out. Maybe you feel like Job, when he talked to God about his life. Here was a guy who could really have gone for those six beers to escape his broken spirit.

> *My spirit is broken,*
> *my days used up,*
> *my grave dug and waiting.*
> *See how these mockers close in on me?*
> *How long do I have to put up with their insolence?*
>
> *O God, pledge your support for me.*
> *Give it to me in writing, with your signature.*
> *You're the only one who can do it!*
> *These people are so useless!*
> *You know firsthand how stupid they can be.*
> *You wouldn't let them have the last word, would you?*
> *Those who betray their own friends*
> *leave a legacy of abuse to their children.*
>
> *God, you've made me the talk of the town—*
>   *people spit in my face;*
> *I can hardly see from crying so much;*
> *I'm nothing but skin and bones.*
> *Decent people can't believe what they're seeing;*
> *the good-hearted wake up and insist I've given up on God.*
>
> *But principled people hold tight, keep a firm grip on life,*
> *sure that their clean, pure hands will get stronger and stronger!*
>
> *Maybe you'd all like to start over,*
> *to try it again, the bunch of you.*
> *So far I haven't come across one scrap*

of wisdom in anything you've said.
My life's about over. All my plans are smashed,
all my hopes are snuffed out—
My hope that night would turn into day,
my hope that dawn was about to break.
If all I have to look forward to is a home in the graveyard,
if my only hope for comfort is a well-built coffin,
If a family reunion means going six feet under,
and the only family that shows up is worms,
Do you call that hope?
Who on earth could find any hope in that?
No. If hope and I are to be buried together,
I suppose you'll all come to the double funeral!
(Job 17)

God goes on to tell Job that he is the hope Job needs. The conversation between God and Job is quite funny, because God presents Job with a situation that's impossible to solve on his own. God asks Job, *"Or can you pull in the sea beast, Leviathan, with a fly rod and stuff him in your creel?"* (Job 41:1) Basically, can you go out on a boat and catch the Lock Ness Monster with a fishing pole? God again asks Job, *"What hope would you have with such a creature? Why, one look at him would do you in!"* (Job 41:9)

Is this not how we feel when we look into the black hole we think we're living in? Do we really think we can get past our own situations? God is essentially saying, "If you can't even look me in the eye, how do you expect to stand up to me? Who can confront me and get away with it? I'm in charge of all this—I run this universe!" Do we take our bad days and blow them out of proportion? Do we think the only way to get beyond our struggles is drugs and alcohol? If so, the question becomes, where are you putting your hope?

Is it in God or in drugs?

I want you to read a poem that was posted on my Your Story page a few years ago. It addresses the very question we've just been looking at—where are you putting your hope?

Only His Blood can heal our wounds.
How did it come to this, how did my eyes not see?
How can I be waking up with scars and bruises instead of joy and life?
When did the dark begin to override the light, and will the light come back?

I believed you. You told me and I believed you.
And now I am here, bruised and scarred, with only the words resonating in my mind (only His blood can heal our wounds, only His blood can heal our wounds).

Oh please, take it back, take me back, make me beautiful.
Make my scars a memory that doesn't burn, and make these bruises the verdict of what was, not what is.
I believed you.

You told me and I believed you.
I want to be whole again.
I want to breathe again.
I want to live again.

I want to wake up tomorrow and these bruises be gone, and these scars never come back.
I am better than this (only His blood can heal our wounds, only His blood can heal our wounds).
You promised me beauty for ashes, beauty for ashes.
Take these ashes and make them beautiful.

They are burnt and bloody and dry, but I know you can make them beautiful.
These ashes are the sin that ate at me, convinced me, lied to me, told me these bruises I deserved.
I believed you. You told me and I believed you.

Make the ashes beautiful (only His blood can heal our wounds, only His blood can heal our wounds).
This is the final show.
This is the last day I wake up like this.

Today I will wear my bruises and scars as a sign, that tomorrow the light will come back... and His blood will heal my wounds...[54]

Where is your hope? Is it in things that can drag us back down, or is it in the blood that can wash us clean?

---

54 Your Story. "His Blood." Date of Access: August 5, 2010 (http://www.yourstory.info/your-stories/2-cutting-a-similar/132-his-blood.html).

IN THE THERAPIST'S OFFICE
Session Six: by Dr. Merry Lin

THIS WEEK, YOU SIT IN THE WAITING ROOM FEELING UPTIGHT, SINCE YOU DIDN'T practice all the things your shrink told you to do from last session. You were just too busy, although a part of you knows you really didn't put a lot of effort into practicing those grounding techniques. Deep down, you questioned whether they could actually work, and besides, it felt so weird to run and get some ice when you were feeling upset. Instead, you ended up cutting after a big blow up with your parents.

You wonder if she'll get mad at you, but you stiffen your spine and think, *Too bad if she doesn't like it.* You're not going to let another adult judge you. As if you don't have enough of that. Your leg starts shaking as you get worked up thinking about your shrink's reaction.

I come out of my office and immediately sense your tension. I wonder what has happened. I see the belligerence on your face and can tell that your back is up for some reason. You come into my office, but you don't look at me as you play with your sleeve. I start with my usual greeting and gentle questions about your week, but you burst out angrily and tell me that you didn't practice your grounding techniques and that you think they're stupid anyway.

When I smile at you and say that it's okay, you look at me in disbelief. I tell you that it takes a lot of baby steps to make changes in your life and it's easy to feel that these changes won't work, but that I'm *proud* of you for being honest with me about how you actually feel.

What the heck?

Your shrink is telling you that you've taken a big step forward because you're actually honest with her about how you *really* feel and not burying it deep inside like you usually do. You also trusted her enough to really speak your mind, which was huge to her. She keeps looking at you warmly, until your anger dissipates completely.

Wow, she reacts totally weird and doesn't get all mad and bossy, like most adults do when you show your anger.

You feel your body relaxing and somehow find yourself promising to give the grounding things a try this week. You feel even more reassured when she tells you that she believes in you and knows that you want to get better, that even when you mess up and cut again, she knows you'll be able to pick yourself up and keep taking those baby steps forward.

You feel better. It feels great that she believes in you, but a part of you thinks she can only say those things because she doesn't know how messed up you really are, and if she knew all the secret, dark thoughts you have inside, she might think otherwise. If she only knew what it's like when you have the desperate urge to hurt yourself. If she only knew about the sick relief you get when you cut. You know that you're totally twisted and bad, especially for someone who's supposed to believe in God.

How can someone who keeps doing something that's so bad ever be anything other than totally messed up?

I can see the doubt in your eyes and my heart hurts for you. If only you could see how truly wonderful you are!

I know how much you beat yourself up for cutting and how that only makes you feel even worse about yourself, how defeated you feel. I'm not going to give up on you and I'll continue to hold onto hope for you, because I believe in you. As I ask you to tell me about your week, I listen with compassion as I hear about your fight with your parents and how you don't feel like they ever hear you, or understand you. I applaud your courage once again for admitting to me that you cut this week, and as I listen I realize that you have a depth to your soul that words cannot ever seem to fully express. I can sense that you're creative, so I hand over some modelling clay and ask you to simply create what it felt like when you had the fight with your parents and when you cut afterward.

I watch quietly as you pick up the clay and squeeze it around in your hands. You do that silently for a few minutes, then pull the clay into pieces, rolling it and thumping the pieces. I can see ideas taking shape in your mind as you work faster and more intentionally. I watch as you fashion a black heart with holes in it and jagged edges, then red drops of blood coming from the edges. I see pieces of the black heart shredded into many pieces, scattered around the heart, and a large knife protruding from the centre. You then build what looks like a brick wall around the heart, enclosing everything. You pause, then make a second wall around the first. Then I watch you fashion a smiling theatre mask which you then attach to the outside perimeter of the second wall.

You sit there and look at your creation for a couple of minutes and I can see you fighting back your emotions. As you try hard to remain stoic, I enter into your pain and gently encourage you to push forward. I ask you to think about what you would call your work of art. After thinking for a few minutes, you tell me that it's called "Twisted Lies." You tell me that it represents all the lies your parents—the whole world, even—told you about love. Lies you live with every day. I wonder out loud about the two walls around the heart and you tell me that it's the only way you can protect yourself. You tell me that no one really wants to know the truth and that you're just going to have to keep faking it. By this time, tears are falling freely down your face. My own eyes fill with tears as I witness your pain, and all I can do is sit with you and keep caring for you as your heart breaks.

As your tears subside, I softly thank you for your honesty and courage, and for trusting me with your pain. I tell you that you haven't scared me away by showing me some of the darkness inside your heart, that I want to keep walking with you through your journey. I then lead you through a grounding exercise to ensure that you're okay before leaving my office. As you complete the exercise, your body relaxes. You nod and reassure me that you're doing okay.

As you leave, you can't believe how tired you feel. You feel a bit flat, but at the same time you feel relieved. It feels good to tell her a little bit of what goes on inside of you and to know that you haven't totally freaked her out.

Boy, this therapy stuff is hard work, but you're starting to believe that it may actually be worth it.

SEVEN
Eating Disorders

eating disorders are a group of serious conditions in which you're so preoccupied with food and weight that you can often focus on little else.

"She's got that disease? ...I always thought they made that up to scare us." Back in the days before the operation, Tally remembered, a lot of people, especially young girls, became so ashamed at being fat that they stopped eating... losing weight until they wound up like this "model." Some even died... That was one of the reasons they'd come up with the operation. No one got the disease anymore, since everyone knew at sixteen they'd turn beautiful.[55]

Scott Westerfeld wrote this passage in the first book of his fictional series *Uglies*, where everyone turns "pretty" at the age of sixteen. The "pretties" live in New Pretty Town and the "uglies" live in Uglyville, waiting for their sixteenth birthday and the operation that will turn them pretty forever. Scott Westerfeld's main character, Tally, must discover

---

55 Westerfeld, Scott. *Uglies* (New York, NY: Simon Pulse, 2011), p. 190.

what "pretty" really means as her world takes a turn when she meets a
friend who doesn't want to become pretty.

> She'd never seen so many wildly different faces before…And
> the bodies. Some were grotesquely fat, or weirdly over muscled,
> or uncomfortably thin, and almost all of them had wrong, ugly
> proportions. But instead of being ashamed of their deformities,
> the people were laughing and kissing and posing…
> "Who are these freaks?"
> "They aren't freaks," Shay said. "The weird thing is, these
> are famous people."
> (…)
> "Yeah. It's scary at first. But the weird thing is, if you keep
> looking at them, you kind of get used to it."[56]

This is such an interesting conversation between the two girls in the
novel, as it's the first time Tally has ever seen "uglies" before they have the
chance to become pretty. The questions that arise here are: What makes
something pretty or ugly? Who determines self-worth and self-image?
How do we determine what look to strive for?

Recently, Stats Canada reported that in women fifteen to twenty-
four years of age, one to two percent struggle with anorexia while three
to five percent are bulimic.[57] The question we need to ask is why there's
such a prevalence for being extremely and oftentimes dangerously thin?
We also need to look at what people define as attractive, and where they
get this understanding. For Tally, it's a team of doctors who performs the
surgery and decide what is pretty. For us, we usually look to others to
determine whether or not we would be considered pretty or ugly. When
that decision is made by others instead of ourselves, our emotional
response can trigger self-injury.

---

56 Ibid., p. 180.

57 Statistics Canada. "Section D - Eating disorders." Date of Access: July 2012 (http://
www.statcan.gc.ca/pub/82-619-m/2012004/sections/sectiond-eng.htm)

The object of desire for a person with an eating disorder or a pattern of disordered eating is food. For the bulimic or the overeater it is the consumption of food. For the anorexic, it is the abstention from food. For the emotional eater, it is the pleasure or calming of food. Each of these limits the freedom to eat in a normal, healthy way. The question becomes, when was desire or control or comfort or calming nailed to food?[58]

When we start to look at food in these ways, we become bound to food. We become its slave and it dictates how we live our lives. A life that is ruled by an eating disorder can be broken by our choices. At some point, we made a choice that food would be our coping mechanism. In order to move beyond our desires, control mechanisms, comforts, or calming agents, we need to figure out why we made that choice. It can be broken.

Blessed be the Lord, the God of Israel;
he came and set his people free.
He set the power of salvation in the center of our lives…
(Luke 1:68–69)

We are told over and over again that when we take our hurt to Jesus, we can be set free. We just need to be willing to break free of our desires and choose a life that's free of bondage. Whether it's cutting, drugs, or food, we can be set free from the pain of it all. That's a great start if you're a Christian with an active prayer life. Some people who are going through an eating disorder will pray for God to release them from the chains of anorexia, but for some this isn't an option. For them, the security and support they'll need is going to come from someone else in their life. Steven Levenkron, in *Anatomy of Anorexia*, dedicates his written word to those individuals who make this type of choice.

---

58 Jantz, Gregory L. and Ann McMurray. *Hope, Help, and Healing for Eating Disorders: A Whole-Person Approach to Treatment of Anorexia, Bulimia, and Disordered Eating.* (Colorado Springs, CO: Waterbrook Press, 2010), p. 82.

To all those brave souls who have given up the only security they knew, for a healthier, frightening, unfamiliar adventure—the quest for a richer life.[59]

Breaking away and forming new habits can be difficult and scary, but the rewards—freedom and relief—are so worth it.

Eating disorders are more than just going on a diet to lose weight or trying to exercise every day. They're extremes in eating behavior—the diet that never ends and gradually gets more restrictive, for example. Or the person who can't go out with friends because he or she thinks it's more important to go running to work off a snack eaten earlier.[60]

BULIMIA

Bulimia nervosa is one of the many potentially life-threatening eating disorders that can be classified as "self-harm." The main characterization of bulimia would be binge eating, followed by a strong compulsion to purge (throw up) what was just consumed. There are many ways in which we purge in our lives, and those may include self-induced vomiting or ingesting large amounts of laxatives to counteract the effects of binge eating. Some people who struggle with bulimia turn to extreme exercise after binge eating in the hopes of burning off the calories that have just entered their body.

Eventually, googling up different weight-loss methods became a habit each night.

No more 10 km runs, they became at least 20 km. Sit-ups before bed. No more sitting still, my legs must jiggle. If I could walk, I could run. After dinner, that's an hour of jogging on the spot with my bedroom door closed so no-one would see me.

---

59 Levenkron, Steven. *Anatomy of Anorexia* (New York, NY: W.W. Norton, 2000), Dedication.

60 Teens Health. "Eating Disorders." Date of Access: March 2012 (http://kidshealth.org/teen/your_mind/mental_health/eat_disorder.html).

It didn't work, I was still as fat as ever. But to my joy, the scales said otherwise. I pinched my waist and cheek fat. Must lose more, I thought to myself. [61]

According to the National Eating Disorders Association, about eighty percent of patients who are diagnosed with bulimia use excessive exercise to control their weight. The majority are women between the ages of fifteen and thirty-five. Bulimia is a way for those struggling with eating disorders to express what they do not want to confront.

Bulimia is often used to express negative emotions or feelings that become too overwhelming to put into words. Through self-induced vomiting or laxative/diuretic abuse, emotions are "purged" out. The temporary release of endorphins misleads you to think this attempt was successful—until the destructive emotional release becomes an overwhelming addiction. [62]

Bulimia and the violent acts it takes to purge the body of what it has consumed is a coping mechanism for emotions that would usually trigger a strong response. Just like shouting out in frustration over an emotional day, bulimia is a way to respond without dealing with the emotional attachment.

BINGE EATING DISORDER
Binge Eating Disorder (BED) has a lot of the same characteristics of bulimia. Most of the motivation that leads someone to this disorder is having our self-worth and self-image compromised by someone close to us. Unlike bulimia, though, BED has no purging actions. The binge eating takes control of the person's life. This is a highly secretive eating disorder, because the amount of food consumed is usually done in seclusion because of the shame felt while eating.

61 Your Story. "Losing Myself." Date of Access: January 2012 (http://www.yourstory.info/your-stories/3-eating-disorders/276-losing-myself-.html).

62 Alcorn, Nancy. *Starved: Mercy for Eating Disorders.* (Enumclaw, WA: WinePress, 2007), p.23.

Anorexia Nervosa

Anorexia nervosa quite often fills voids in the self-injurer's life that they don't want to deal with. It's also a part of a sufferer's need to take control of an area of their life, as they feel like the rest of their life is not within their control. Anorexia is more often less about the food that's not being consumed and more about what the person is trying to avoid thinking about. The truth is, eating disorders are much more complicated than that. Steven Levenkron, in *Anatomy of Anorexia*, breaks the progression of anorexia into four stages, each with its own set of consequences. First, I think it's important to touch on the medical issues that break down the body.

> Many descriptions of anorexia take a medical standpoint, detailing the effects that that the disorder's progress has on the body. Medically, anorexia is characterized by weight loss, followed by lowered body temperature, lowered blood pressure, slowed heart rate, loss of menses, thinning of hair, fatigue, and other signs of malnutrition. As the anorexic continues to lose weight, new symptoms develop and intensify. The last, lethal stage for anorexic patients is failure of the liver, kidneys, and finally the heart. [63]

The food and weight-related issues are symptoms of a deeper hurt: these can be related to almost anything else that we talk about in this book—depression, loneliness, insecurity, the pressure to be perfect, or feeling out of control. One thirteen-year-old girl wrote to me saying that she started starving herself because she felt the need to have control over something in her life while everything else was spiralling out of control.

> I just started going down hill and became depressed. I started cutting. But after my swimming coach saw and told my mom, I stopped for the most part. Then I was falling apart and

---

63 Levenkron, Steven. *Anatomy of Anorexia*. (New York, NY: W.W. Norton, 2000), p. 33.

needed something I could be in control of, so I started starving myself, eating as little as possible. After a month I had lost over 20 pounds and people started to notice, so I started eating a little more so people didn't get so suspicious.[64]

These deeper issues, regarding why we fall into eating disorders, cannot be solved through any amount of dieting or consumption of food. This girl isn't going to solve her issues through not eating because, like she wrote, it brought attention to her and she saw the need to change in order to cover up the deeper issues and keep questions about her feelings away. She wasn't ready to open up and wrestle through the complex emotions at work. Eating disorders can only be solved once we address the root issues.

Levenkron's four stages allow for a greater understanding of the mindset of the self-injurer. The first stage is a sense of achievement that comes with weight loss. Levenkron states,

> …it is in line with the trend most girls adopt who consider gaining weight unacceptable and an enemy to be fought with an all-out assault.[65]

In the beginning, anorexia is seen by most girls to be a simple solution to weight loss. They see losing weight as the target; it becomes an all-or-nothing mentality for them.

The second stage is characterized by a compulsion to lose weight. This compulsion takes over every facet of life. This decision, to base all life around losing weight, establishes a life that is full of fear. They are scared to eat, scared to gain weight, scared their metabolism might slow down. All these fears and decisions create a secret compulsion to

---

64 Your Story. "My thoughts haven't won yet! I'm holding on with the help of God!" Date of Access: January 2012 (http://www.yourstory.info/your-stories/4-suicide-a-depression/215-my-thoughts-havent-won-yet-im-holding-on-with-the-help-of-god. html).

65 Levenkron, Steven. *Anatomy of Anorexia*. (New York, NY: W.W. Norton, 2000), p. 34.

hide what's really going on in their lives. They hide it behind the only solutions they know.

> How is she to find shelter and security from these fears? Eating even less and exercising have become her only solutions to achieve security. Her obsession with achieving security from these fears leads to ever-expanding protective behaviours she feels compelled to perform. [66]

Levenkron's third stage begins with an assertive new voice that the anorexic did not know he or she had. They are no longer concerned when family members or friends begin to question their massive weight loss, because they have, maybe for the first time, been purposely defying the wishes of those who care about them most.

> The disease has given her a new sense of power she did not anticipate when she first began to lose weight. Her special thinness has become one with her special assertiveness. To give up one would be to lose the other.[67]

For parents, this is usually when they begin to see how strong a hold anorexia has on their child. There is a strong change in the assertiveness of the person's voice that parents may be frightened to question, in fear that it will lead to more anorexic behaviour.

The last stage doesn't bring about any new behaviours but is identified by a strong exhibitionist attitude toward weight loss. They start to show off what they believe every other person cannot pull off: being thin and extreme weight control.

> This exhibitionism becomes a weapon—an outward declaration of war against other girls and women (note: it can be men) to make a statement about who has the most willpower, who can best control her appetite…

---

66 Ibid, p. 37.
67 Ibid., p. 39

She has now achieved what she believes to be her identity, a way of being known as special, as defined. This pseudo-identity fills in the emptiness she has secretly felt about herself for some time.[68]

They start to wear tighter and shorter clothes so they can show off how in control of their weight they are. They believe everyone else is jealous of their success. The danger here is that anorexia—or rather, being thin—becomes their identity. They find themselves in something new while running away from the emotions that drove them towards anorexia. Anorexia now defines them.

Anorexia nervosa is usually characterized in two ways. Anorexic behaviour is controlled either through restricting the intake of calories and food, or through purging any calories consumed through vomiting or laxatives. Anorexic mentality is a constant battle. It never leaves. It doesn't simply fade away in the busyness of a typical day. It lingers in their thoughts; it becomes their thought process. It starts with a refusal to maintain a healthy body weight, because they don't see themselves as healthy. They see that little bit of skin they can grab on their waist and try to purge their body of it.

> I used to think I was beautiful. I was a carefree and happy girl. Until I wasn't. I would look in the mirror and see fat. And ugly. And loser. I was never good enough. I'm still trying hard to see the beauty everyone else says they see in me.
> - Anonymous

The purging isn't seen as a successful way to lose weight in all instances, though. It can often be seen as a failure to succeed at maintaining the ideal weight, failure to maintain a strict diet, which often leaves one with feelings of shame and hunger.

Portia de Rossi describes the process like this:

"I hated purging. It was punishment that I couldn't stick to a diet," she says. "I hated binging, [but] binging momentarily gave me relief, because I'd been starving, really. Psychologically, I just wanted to fill the void. But the purging, the purging

---

68 Ibid.

made me feel more pathetic than just having failed yet another diet."[69]

Their thoughts are driven by fear of that little bit of skin, by fear that it will grow and become the focal point of their self-image and the image everyone else sees.

"Eww. You're ugly... have you seen yourself in the mirror lately? Look at that... ugh, you're disgusting. You really should lose some weight."

These thoughts rolled through my head day and night. Before my feet even touched the floor in the morning, I was already criticizing myself. Throughout the day even the smell of food would make me shiver because it reminded me of how ugly I was. I wasn't always like this...[70]

This constant battle leaves people with a distorted version of themselves and their own self-worth based on what they see in the mirror, or the offhand comments of those closest to them.

This makes mealtimes stressful. The very fact that you cannot eat becomes the very thought you keep coming back to, keep dwelling on.

Now, it might sound insane to you that I speak of anorexia as if it were human. As if it were a flesh and blood friend. And I guess that does sound a little absurd... but it's reality. I would talk to Ana out loud. I would scream at her and throw things at her; I would laugh with her and celebrate with her. After all... she was my only friend.

The only way for me to keep Ana as my friend was to not eat. If I was around food... it was a living hell.

69 Oprah.com. "The Secret That Nearly Killed Her." Date of Access: March 2012 (http://www.oprah.com/oprahshow/The-Secret-That-Nearly-Killed-Portia-de-Rossi#ixzz1qEcic8YR).

70 Your Story. "Painful Relief... and Ana." Date of Access: March 2012 (http://www.yourstory.info/your-stories/3-eating-disorders/199-painful-reliefand-ana.html).

You can't eat that... you just CAN'T. If you eat it you'll hurt Ana's feelings and she won't want to be your friend. You don't want to hurt her feelings... she loves you. She LOVES you. Listen to her.[71]

This constant battle over thoughts about eating take the place of old hobbies, friends, and family as every moment of every day becomes consumed with thinking of better diets and shedding extra pounds.

The worst part? The day when I had gained a pound and six ounces. I cried, curled up in a ball on the bathroom floor. But I had to take control. So I crawled over to the toilet, and shoved my fingers down my throat. You know what happened next. This sickening existence, this pitiful routine, went on for three months.[72]

That story comes from a girl whose dream was to be a dancer, a dream that was stalled when the disease took her beyond what's considered beautiful in today's cultural norms.

But in that instant something happened. I stared at the little pouch of fat on my stomach, at my wide thighs. Fear crawled inside me, whispering in my ear. "You must do something about this!" it hissed. "You can't be average! You can't be fat!"[73]

EDNOS

Eating disorders not otherwise specified (EDNOS) were introduced to the public in the early 90s but haven't really been a part of the eating disorder discussion. Such discussions usually drift towards either

---

71 Ibid.

72 Your Story. "A Dancer's Dream." Date of Access: March 2012 (http://www.yourstory. info/your-stories/3-eating-disorders/218-a-dancers-dream.html).

73 Ibid.

anorexia or bulimia. Here are the EDNOS that need to be added to our knowledge about eating disorders.

EDNOS	Definition*
Orthorexia	A fixation with healthy or righteous eating. Orthorexics often eat only organic foods, eliminate entire food groups, or refuse to eat anything that isn't "pure."
Pregorexia	Extreme dieting and exercising while pregnant to avoid gaining the twenty-five to thirty-five pounds of weight doctors usually recommend.
Anorexia Athletica	An addiction to exercise.
Drunkorexia	Restricting food intake in order to reserve those calories for alcohol and binge drinking.

*Deam, Jean. Women's Health "New Eating Disorders." Date of Access: Aug. 2012. (http://www.womenshealthmag.com/health/new-eating-disorders)

IN THE THERAPIST'S OFFICE
Session Seven: by Dr. Merry Lin

IT HAS BEEN A PRETTY GOOD WEEK, ALTHOUGH YOU HAD A COUPLE OF ROUGH moments; it was exam week and you were totally stressed. You were especially stressed over your math exam, but it helped that you were able to email your shrink to vent about how you were feeling. You surprised yourself with how much detail you wrote in your email to her, but then again, you've always found it a lot easier to open up in writing than in person. You instantly felt better when she replied and said a few encouraging things to you.

You see your shrink's smiling face as she opens her office door. You have to admit that you're kind of looking forward to seeing her today. It feels pretty good to be with someone who seems to get you and not judge you, or tell you what to do. You still wonder at all the crazy things she does, as it sure isn't what you thought would happen when your parents dragged you to see her. But whatever, you're sure she knows what she's doing. Either that or she's just crazier than you are!

You spend some time chatting and find yourself laughing as she tells you a funny story about her dog and the underwear he managed to swallow. You can't stop laughing as she tells you about the loud and smelly farts he blessed her with for two weeks before he managed to finally discharge the underwear from his stomach. The way she hoots as she laughs makes you laugh even more.

I love seeing your eyes light up as you laugh! You are such a delight to me and I love hanging out with you. You are so teachable that it is a joy to be with you. Today, I want to give you even more tools to calm yourself down and cope with the turmoil of life. And so I talk to you about the benefits of laughter. You tell me that you secretly love to watch Sponge Bob with your younger brother, so I encourage you to consider that a "grounding" technique when you're feeling bad. I tell you that interrupting your dark thoughts with light-hearted humour can help distract you in a positive way. I tell you about the physiological benefits of laughter.

Today we're going to do something called the "Safe Place" exercise. I explain to you that it's a great mental exercise that can automatically bring you to a state of relaxation and calmness, especially when you're feeling anxious or upset. I talk about what happens physiologically in your brain as you do this exercise; just by thinking about your safe place, your brain will recall all the good feelings of relaxation associated with it. I ask you to get yourself into a comfortable position and close your eyes. I then ask you to think about a place where you feel the safest and most comfortable and at ease. As you think about it, I add that it can be a real place you have actually been to, or it can be a place from your imagination.

You think about it for a moment and then tell your shrink that it's on the white sand beaches in the Bahamas where you went on vacation with your family earlier that year. She asks you to imagine yourself there and to tell her in detail what you actually see. As you talk about the sand, the water, the trees, the sun and clouds, and the birds flying, you picture it in your mind. She then tells you to describe what you hear and you tell her about the sound of the water, the voices in the distance, the calypso music, and the sound of palm leaves rustling in the wind. As you go on to describe everything you smell and feel, it feels so real to you that it's almost like you're there. She reminds you throughout the exercise to keep breathing deeply. Her voice remains soft and quiet throughout. You find yourself relaxing more and more as you focus on the scene in your mind. You're feeling so relaxed that you're almost ready to fall asleep.

She then asks you to describe how you feel right now; the words *calm*, *peaceful*, and *happy* come to mind. She gets you to do a body scan to see if there's any tension there, but nope, it's all good. Finally, she asks you to think of a name for this place. After some thought, you tell her it's your Happy Place. You know it's kind of cheesy, but it's only for you to know, so whatever. She asks you to keep picturing the scene in your mind and to say "Happy Place" to yourself a few times. Afterward, she tells you to practice going to your Happy Place a couple times over the week to train your brain to quickly bring on those good feelings.

Wow, that was really cool. You like this exercise a lot and decide that you're definitely going to do it more often. You leave her office feeling really good.

EIGHT
I Am Healthy

disney star Demi Lovato is one of many celebrities who have admitted to suffering through issues with self-harm in one form or another. She entered a rehab facility in 2010 so that she could find a safe place to deal with her lifelong battle with eating disorders.

These words pierced like a knife... but I was always taught to keep my feelings to myself. No one would care or listen to me anyways. So I just play along with them, laugh at their jokes, play around by stuffing more food in my mouth, living up to what they expected me to be. I mean, yeah these words hurt... but I would never be anorexic. Never.
- Anonymous

But I will deal with it for the rest of my life because it is a life-long disease. I don't think there's going to be a day when I don't think about food or my body, but I'm living with it, and I wish I could tell young girls to find their safe place and stay with it.[74]

---

74 Radar. "Demi Lovato On Her Eating Disorder: 'It's a Life-Long Disease.'" Date of Access: April 2012 (www.radaronline.com/exclusives/2011/04/demi-lovato-her-eating-disorder-its-a-life-long-disease).

Here is a talented and beautiful girl who has dealt with bullying, which led to hurting with no clear outlet for her feelings. Her message is to find a safe place for that outlet so that the emotions and hurt don't build up and lead to self-injury.

It's very crucial that you get your feelings out—but don't ever inflict harm on your own body because your body is so sacred.[75]

We are in a position of authority in our kids' lives. It is our responsibility to allow them to feel safe enough to share their feelings with someone who shows genuine care and regard for how they feel. If we aren't providing a safe place, they will look for another outlet for their emotions. The danger is that the outlet could become self-injury, a release of emotional pain through bodily harm.

Demi Lovato isn't the only celebrity who has dealt with this issue. Actress Portia de Rossi has openly talked about her battle with eating disorders in her very raw and blunt memoir, *Unbearable Lightness: A Story of Loss and Gain*. In an interview on Oprah, Portia talked about how and why she relied on purging her body for modelling gigs.

Portia says she went on her first diet when she was 12 years old. She had started modeling and had to call an agency to tell them her measurements. She says when she told them her bust was 32 inches, her waist 27 inches and her hips 37 inches, the modeling booker paused and said, "Just tell people you're 34-24-35." Portia says that was the moment she decided she had to diet to be able to work, because her body wasn't good enough the way it was.

"After the diet, I'd do the job, I'd binge, and then I'd have a few days to get the weight off before I did the next job," says Portia. "But as the jobs got booked back-to-back, I had to get the weight off faster, so I used laxatives, I used diuretics, and

---

75 Ibid.

then when that didn't work, I was forced to purge… to throw up." [76]

Self-injury isn't an issue that affects only one group of people; it can affect anyone, because it relies on emotion and how an individual releases those emotions.

Eating disorders do a number on the systems of our body. It's not as simple as shedding a couple of pounds; every time we purge our body of the nutrients it needs, it reacts in different ways.

For someone with bulimia, there's the danger of severe dehydration through the expulsion of bodily fluids, whether that's by vomiting or the use of laxatives. There's also a strong chance that they'll suffer from tooth decay from all of the acidic liquid that is produced from purging, as well as ulcers, or suffering from acid reflux. Our throats aren't designed to take constant purging and will usually become hoarse and sore.

The health risks of bulimia run from problems with the brain to the stomach; one's skin and digestive track can be affected as well. A person's cheeks swell and their teeth can decay, leading to extreme sensitivity from exposed nerves, making hot and cold foods torturous for years to come. Throats and oesophaguses are in danger of rupturing due to the stress of prolonged vomiting and acid build-up. The extreme pressure from prolonged vomiting can also cause blood vessels to pop in a person's eyes, making them look bloodshot all the time.

They can also suffer from irregular bowel movements and diarrhoea. Vomiting, laxatives, and diuretics can cause electrolyte imbalances in the body, most commonly in the form of low potassium levels. Low potassium levels trigger a wide range of symptoms ranging from lethargy and cloudy thinking to an irregular heartbeat and death. Chronically low levels of potassium can also result in kidney failure.

76 Oprah.com. "The Secret That Nearly Killed Her." Date of Access: March 2012 (http://www.oprah.com/oprahshow/The-Secret-That-Nearly-Killed-Portia-de-Rossi#ixzz1qEcic8YR).

DRUGS AND ALCOHOL

In reality, our first drink or exposure to drugs will probably come from one of our best friends, someone who has already made some really bad choices and is now trying to justify their choices by asking/pressuring you into making a similar decision.

I still talk with parents who think that the first time their child gets asked to do drugs will be from that weird guy downtown, who will jump out and take advantage of the innocence of a child. More likely, it will come from a close friend.

As parents and leaders, we need to be aware not only that our youth are drinking and doing drugs, but also address the root issues of why they're using these substances. Perhaps it's a simple mood adjustment, to help them relax before a big test or game, to help them feel more creative, or to move out of the box they feel stuck in. Or it could be as something as simple as drinking to alleviate the boredom of everyday life. Whatever the case, drugs and alcohol aren't the real issue. The substances are escape from something they feel there is no escape from.

Using substances as a way to forget or move past strong emotions is so dangerous. What happens when the usual amount of beer or marijuana doesn't cut it anymore? Do you move to a new drug, or amp up the amount of alcohol you consume? The ease with which a problem or addiction can arise from this type of usage is hard to wrap our minds around. As adults, many times we don't do enough to show that alcohol isn't the answer to life's curveballs.

Think about it. When was the last time you said something like, "I could use a drink right now"? When was the last time you told a joke about some wild party or work function that was filled with the over-consumption of alcohol? The way we treat alcohol in our own homes is how our children will treat alcohol in their friend's homes.

We are so arrogant, both as a society and as individuals, that we watch TV shows like *Intervention* and think that it will never be us. How do we know for sure?

No one ever gets to the age of twenty-five, thirty-five, or even forty and thinks, *Man, I wish I did more drugs in school.* If we wanted to be twenty-five years old and be a drug addict or alcoholic, we would know what to do given hindsight: drink more and experiment with harder and harder drugs. If, however, you want to be twenty-five and graduating from university or college without any dependencies, you can stay away from anything that might hurt your future. Reverse the plan you've found yourself in and move into the future you want for yourself.

A survey done by the Youth Risk Behaviour Survey (YRBS) of ninth- to twelfth-grade students showed that seventy percent of the students had at least tried alcohol. Twenty percent of those students had tried alcohol before the age of thirteen, and just under forty percent of those students had drank at least one drink within the thirty days that the survey was taken. Twenty percent also admitted to having repeated drinks on at least one day.[77] The introduction of alcohol into our lives starts early. This is a shock for many adults, but we need to get move past our ignorance and move into productive and open conversations in the home about how alcohol is used by everyone, including adults.

In the same survey, it was reported that twenty-five percent of students were offered, sold, or given an illegal drug by someone on school property.[78]

Moving past addiction is a hard step that can only be established by the user. They need to want to make a change and address the reasons behind the substance abuse before any progress can be made. That might mean seeing a counsellor, going to a group like Alcohol Anonymous, or checking into a rehab facility that includes counselling sessions.

Eminem released an album called *Recovery* which had some great messages for anyone looking to make positive changes in their lives. The video for "Not Afraid," in particular, has a positive message when it comes to addictions and overcoming those addictions. In the song, Eminem talks about why he made the decision to clean himself up and move past his addictions.

---

77 CDC. "Trends in the Prevalence of Alcohol Use National YRBS: 1991–2011." Date of Access: July 2012 (www.cdc.gov/healthyyouth/yrbs/pdf/us_alcohol_trend_YRBS. pdf).

78 CDC. "Trends in the Prevalence of Tobacco, Alcohol, and Illegal Drug Use on School Property National YRBS: 1991–2011." Date of Access: July 2012 (www.cdc. gov/healthyyouth/yrbs/pdf/us_taodu_trend_YRBS.pdf).

It was my decision to get clean. I did it for me. Admittedly, I probably did it subliminally for you so I could come back a brand new me. You helped see me through and don't even realize what you did. Believe me you, I been through the ringer, but they can do little to the middle finger. I think I got a tear in my eye. I feel like the king of my world. Haters can make like bees with no stingers, and drop dead. No more beef flingers, no more drama from now on. I promise to focus solely on handling my responsibilities as a father, so I solemnly swear to always treat this roof like my daughters and raise it. You couldn't lift a single shingle on it. Cause the way I feel, I'm strong enough to go to the club or the corner pub and lift the whole liquor counter up 'cause I'm raising the bar. I shoot for the moon, but I'm too busy gazing at stars, I feel amazing and...[79]

The video for "Not Afraid" is so compelling because it deals with imagery that helps portray not only his long battle to overcome addictions, but also how difficult the process really can be.

Images of Eminem breaking through a brick wall further carry the "recovery" theme, symbolizing his battle against alcohol addiction and prescription drugs. Other signs of the rapper's desire for change: a promise to never let his fans down again and "to focus solely on handling my responsibilities as a father."[80]

Moving past addictions and looking at the responsibilities life has laid before our very feet is in integral part of the reverse engineering lifestyle. The responsibilities and goals we place in our lives take the place of the substances we leave behind.

---

79 Eminem, Kobe, P!nk, Lil Wayne, and Rihanna. "Recovery." Santa Monica, CA: Aftermath Records, 2010.

80 Culture and Media Institute. "Culture and Media Institute." Date of Access: June 8, 2010 (http://www.cultureandmediainstitute.org/articles/2010/20100608170031.aspx).

IN THE THERAPIST'S OFFICE
Session Eight: by Dr. Merry Lin

TODAY, YOU WAIT A BIT ANXIOUSLY BECAUSE THE SHRINK TOLD YOU LAST SESSION that you were going to do something called "sand tray therapy." When she described it to you, it sounded kind of fun, but when she told you it was a way for you to tell your story, your stomach felt kind of jumpy, like maybe you're going to go places you don't really want to. Maybe you'll have to talk about some of the bad things in your life you don't want to think about. You are, however, starting to feel like you can trust her, so you agree.

When she comes to the waiting room to get you, you make a nervous joke that it's time to play in the sand. She laughs warmly, then takes you to a different room. As you walk in, your eyes take in all the different miniatures and figurines lined up along the bookshelf. In spite of yourself, you are totally fascinated with everything you see. There are all sorts of people, animals, insects, furniture, scary creatures, angels, fences, buildings, weapons… even tiny plastic food and bottles of booze. You walk in further and you see a flat box filled with sand on the table.

I smile as I see your face and can tell you're interested in what you see. I give you a few moments to look around and then ask you to simply create your world. I remind you that there are no right or wrong answers, that this is a creative way to share a tiny bit of your world with me. I encourage you to pick whatever items attract your interest without worrying about giving it too much thought. I watch you wander around the room, picking up different items and gathering them into your arms. You seem to be very thoughtful but also purposeful.

I then watch as you begin to place the items you've picked into the sand. I see that you've picked up a little girl and put beside her a puppy dog. Right next to the little girl, lying face down and partially buried in the sand, is a Mr. T. action figure. You then place a baby boy figurine behind the little girl. I notice that you've got a headless queen figurine placed far away with its back to the little girl. Hidden at her feet away from the little girl are tiny bottles of alcohol. You then place a figure of a man wearing a suit and holding a briefcase; he is off in the corner of the sand tray, facing away from the others, looking off into the distance.

You look at what you've done so far and it doesn't feel quite right. So, you go back to the bookshelf and pick up a gargoyle, placing it right behind the little girl. Next, you pick up a bracelet of bright red beads and place it around the little girl, with a knife plunging into the sand. You then grab the church and place it into another corner of the tray facing the little girl. That doesn't quite feel right, either, so you pick up the jail cell and place it underneath the church. You nod; that feels right. You sit down and just stare at your tray, feeling completely numb.

You then look up at me and I ask you to tell me about the tray. You hesitate, but okay, here it goes.

You point to the little girl and say that it is you with your puppy, Clover. Your little brother is the baby hiding behind your back and you tell me that you've always felt like it's your job to protect and take care of him. You smile as you talk about him and I can tell he's really special to you. You then point to Mr. T. and say that he is your big brother, who always bullied you when you were growing up, but at the same time you know that deep down he's a good guy. You tell me that he was always off getting into fights at bars and your parents were always rescuing him out of one thing or another. I see the sadness in your face as you tell me that he's now in jail after having been caught trying to rob a store. You tell me that the headless queen is your mom, who always hides in her room drinking booze, thinking that somehow no one knows what's going on. And your dad, the figurine with the briefcase, is never there, as he's always travelling for work. Finally, in the corner is the church, which is like a jail cell because it's about all the rules you keep messing up; you always feel so ashamed and condemned at church; you feel like you can never be yourself there.

Your face looks empty as you tell me all of this, but I can sense your isolation and loneliness. No one is looking at you except your older brother and he's the one you describe as the bully. I then point to the gargoyle and the red beads and knife and softly ask you to tell me about that. You hesitate, and I can see you fighting the emotions. I wait without saying a word.

A tear begins rolling down your cheek, followed by another one. You sniff, and with a quavering voice you point to the gargoyle and tell me that that is the real you, ugly and evil. As you look at the gargoyle and the "bloody" beads, you break down and begin to cry. I feel very sad for you, but I also know that you're finally getting a chance to tell me your story, so I listen as you tell me of your shame, loneliness, and feelings of abandonment, all without using any words. I can tell that you feel like no one is there for you and that you're left on your own to deal with overwhelming pain and sorrow. Even sadder for me are the people who are supposed to protect you but aren't there, and the church you go to, which hasn't taught you about God's love and grace for you.

When the shrink asks you to give your tray a title, you pause and then tell her that it is "Living Hell." She tells you that she hears you and that she can see the loneliness and abandonment you've been feeling, how you've felt abandoned to deal with the pain in your life alone. You nod, your heart aching even more as you hear her empathetic words.

Can you… should you tell her?

What will she think of your worst secret, the thing that makes you feel so bad and dirty?

Can you do it?

You have to. The secret is killing you.

With your heart pounding so hard you can barely hear yourself speak, you tell her that when you were a little girl, your older brother was left alone to babysit you. You don't remember everything that happened, but you remember that he touched you in your private parts and you remember feeling really scared. You were probably only three years old, but you know it went on for three years until you were finally able to go to school full-time.

You are petrified at what your shrink is going to say because you have *never* told anyone about this. You finally look at her and you're shocked to see the tears in her eyes and the look of tenderness on her face as she murmurs your name and tells you that she feels very, very sad for you. As she looks at you with such compassion, you break down even more and start crying so hard, you feel like you're wailing. You feel like you've never cried this hard in your life and it feels like you'll never be able to stop. The shrink asks if it's okay for her to hug you and you nod, so she sits next to you and wraps her arms tight around you. You bury your head in her shoulder and feel the warmth of her arms, the sobs beginning to slow. After a while, you lift your head and sit back, sniffing and hiccupping. She takes your hand and squeezes it, then goes back to sit in her chair while you blow your nose and clean yourself up.

You feel slightly embarrassed, but at the same time it feels like a huge weight has been lifted off your shoulder. Finally your secret is out and everything is okay. Actually, better than okay, because you know your shrink is on your side and is doing everything she can to help you heal. You know that what happened to you wasn't your fault, and her words of empathy only confirm it for you. You knew that, but now you actually believe it. The shrink leads you through a grounding exercise to make sure you're safe, but you know you're going to be okay.

NINE
Anxiety and Depression

Being depressed is bad enough in itself, but being a depressed Christian is worse. And being a depressed Christian in a church full of people who do not understand depression is like a little taste of hell.[81]

—John Lockley

For many years, I longed for March 2012. I was completing a Master's degree at Wheaton Grad School in Chicago, speaking hundreds of times a year and still trying to balance this with being a father and husband. I had my final class in January 2012 and received my notice that I passed the course in the last few days of February. On March 1, everything collapsed when I began to wake up an hour early everyday. Instead of waking up at seven, I would wake up at six. It wasn't a big issue, but then it began to happen earlier and earlier.

Five.

Four, and then it was…

Three.

---

81 Murray, David P. *Christians Get Depressed Too: Hope and Help for Depressed People* (Grand Rapids, MI: Reformation Heritage Books, 2010), Kindle edition.

Finally, when I began to wake up at two, things started to get weird for me. My sleep patterns were badly out of whack. I would wake up thinking it was morning, but it was the middle of the night. I was tired all time, agitated.

One day, I was speaking in Chatham, Ontario, not too far from Toronto. Right in the middle of one of my talks, I felt like I was about to pass out. It was one of the weirdest feelings I'd ever had. The world starting to twist and twirl around me. I broke out into a sweat and goose bumps appeared on my arms and legs.

I asked the youth pastor for a short break. That's when I sensed something was really wrong. I found myself a couple of minutes later with a juice box in my hand as someone gave me something to eat. This was the first time in fifteen years that I'd been forced to stop and take a break for any reason during one of my speaking engagements.

The next morning, I was scheduled to speak with a group of parents at the same church, but I felt the need to cancel. I was dizzy and had no idea what was going on. I went to the front of the church to pack up my laptop. After sitting and talking to a few people for about ten minutes, I decided that if I could just stay exactly where I was, except at the front of the stage, I think I could try to do the talk. I made it through, but I still didn't feel like myself.

In the weeks that followed, I saw a number of doctors and was given sleeping pills to help with the sleepless nights. Unfortunately, they didn't result in better sleeps, even after going through six different brands. I still woke up a half-dozen times every night. I also tried a sleep clinic. I had a CAT scan done as well at a local hospital. All these tests came back negative, which was great, but still left me with no answers.

I figured I was okay to travel to Alberta to speak at Camp Caroline, just over an hour northwest of Calgary. I remember feeling off during the flight, and when we landed I had to rest multiple times on benches before I got my luggage. I picked up my rental car and started driving. As I drove through the town of Airdrie, I spotted a sign with a large "H" on it for hospital. I pulled over and wondered if I should go in. At this point, I literally thought I was dying. My heart was pounding out of my chest and my head felt like it was about to explode. My emotions were all over the map and I found myself crying multiple times.

I decided to drive on to the camp.

The next morning, I got up to speak after a really bad night's sleep. I tried to have breakfast and still felt sick, so I thought I would lie down for thirty minutes before my first session. As I lay on my bunk, I experienced something completely new to me. I began to panic. I look back and realize this was the first of five large panic attacks I suffered over the next few months. I talked to the people from the retreat and said I had to leave. In my panic, I left the event and drove to the airport, desperate to get home.

When I got home, I went to the doctor again and went through yet another round of sleeping medication. I booked an appointment with another sleep specialist in Toronto, as well as with a psychiatrist in my hometown. Between all these tests, I tried a couple of local speaking dates. Even though I was able to finish them, the dizziness and feelings of just being "off" wouldn't leave.

However, I decided to go on tour in Windsor, Ontario to speak at ten Catholic schools. The first talk went great and I made it through… but then the second one came. I was in front of seven or eight hundred students when the world spun again. So, there I was in the middle of one of my talks, and in the back of my head I was trying to figure out what I should do when I passed out.

Should I just lie on the ground in front of the audience?

It was one of those moments I'll never forget. The world was spinning out of control, yet I was somehow able to finish.

I went back to my hotel to take a nap, as my eyes and brain were screaming for sleep. I just couldn't sleep. Every time I closed my eyes, I thought I would enter into a REM state while I was still awake. Instead of experiencing darkness as I closed my eyes, I would see flashes of light, almost like a strobe light was penetrating my eyelids. I wasn't able to eat any dinner that night because of how sick I felt. I don't know if I actually got any sleep that night at all.

The next morning, while getting ready to go out for my next talk, I called my wife, Dawn.

"I don't feel right," I told her. "What do I do?"

In the back of my head, I knew it wasn't fair to put this on her, but I didn't know who to call. I was alone.

She told me I had to make a choice. If I could speak, then speak, but if I thought I couldn't get through my next talk, I should cancel.

Ten minutes later, I found myself on the side of the road in my car, crying. I remember saying out loud, "What is going on with me?

This was just not me.

I knew at that point I wasn't okay. I wasn't all right. I felt broken.

I called the school and cancelled my talk that morning. Then I called the tour organizer and cancelled the rest of my dates.

After returning home, I went back to my doctor and was prescribed more medication. This time, he diagnosed me with anxiety and put me on anxiety medication during the day and some heavier anxiety/depression medication at nighttime. I was now among the millions of people worldwide who struggle with anxiety and depression. Steve and Robyn Bloem, in their book *Broken Minds*, speak about how many people, including Steve, struggle with a mental illness.

> One in five people experiences depression, and one in ten experience a panic attack at some stage in his life. An estimated 121 million people worldwide suffer from depression. Studies show that 5.8 percent of men and 9.5 percent of women will experience a depressive episode in any given year.[82]

The Canadian statistics for anxiety and depression aren't that far off from the Bloems' analysis in their book. A nationwide survey of Canadian youth by Statistics Canada found that 6.5%—more than a quarter million youth and young adults between the ages of fifteen and twenty-four—met the criteria for major depression in the past year.[83]

---

82 Bloem, Steve and Robin. *Broken Minds* (Grand Rapids, MI: Kregal, 2005), pp. 54–55.

83 Public Health Agency of Canada. "The Chief Public Health Officer's Report on the State of Public Health in Canada, 2011." Date of Access: March 2012 (http://www.phac-aspc.gc.ca/cphorsphc-respcacsp/2011/cphorsphc-respcacsp-06-eng.php).

Michael Landsburg from TSN and host of *Off the Record* has made public his personal battle with depression over the last few years. He speaks towards many of the fears those who have mental illness face when they first look for help.

> There's this belief that you can tell people who are depressed. But everyone with depression becomes a good actor... Nobody really conveys the depth of their pain all the time.[84]

He also sees that there's a personal battle over whether the person sees mental health as a weakness, or if they're open to talk about it. If the viewpoint is that mental health illnesses are a sign of personal weakness, they'll have a harder time conveying or sharing their true feelings to anyone.

> One of the problems with depression—and one of the reasons why there is this stigma and perception that depression is about personal weakness—is that you can't really tell someone what it feels like. You end up using words that are really ambiguous.[85]

If there's no one to talk to or listen to, or you just aren't ready to open up about your hurt yet, his interview sounds a note of caution.

> "Right away you believe it's your fault," he says. "I found, as time went on, I fell deeper and deeper in and, instead of working my way out of it, I was working my way deeper into it."[86]

---

84 The Saturday Ticket. "Michael Landsberg's Journey To 'Depression's Hell'" Date of Access: July 2012 (http://sports.sympatico.ca/home/thesaturdayticket/opinions/michael_landsbergs_journey_to_depressions_hell/7df64a9d).

85 Ibid.

86 Ibid.

As we hold onto our hurts and secrets, we only push healing that much farther away.

It was interesting for me, someone who speaks on issues like anxiety and depression, to suddenly be diagnosed with that. Over the next two weeks, while I adjusted to my new medication, I cancelled another speaking tour, this one in the Ottawa area. I couldn't do it; the medication made me sleepy, and I still couldn't shake the dizziness when standing for long periods of time.

That takes me to the present day. So far, I've had to cancel 120 speaking dates, and I may have to cancel more as I work through these struggles. This continues to be an interesting journey for me. I'm starting to feel better during the mornings, though I experience bad headaches in the early afternoons that don't go away. Presently, I've been off speaking for six months. I still struggle with anxiety and I'm working with a psychiatrist and psychologist to help get me back on-track. It's a slow, long, dark journey.

I'm just starting to understand the role of anxiety and depression in my own life. I still don't understand it, since I don't personally have a history that lends itself to anxiety. I have a great life. Nonetheless, I struggle with for sleep and anxiety. I have good days and bad days. I've been able to start running again, but my first three-kilometre run knocked me out of commission for nearly three days. I've slowly been running further and feeling better. I pray daily for strength, peace of mind, sleep, and less anxiety so I can soon get back to speaking.

In church, we often talk about brokenness. For the first time in my life, I understand that. It's weird coming to a place where you feel alone and uncertain about your future, to feel mortal. There were times when I was alone in a hotel and didn't know what to say or how to explain how I felt. I just didn't know what to do.

I felt hopeless.

That's not a nice place to be. I prayed, I read my Bible, and I talked to my friends, but I didn't know what was going on. I felt like my ministry, which I'd spent fifteen years building, was slipping through my fingers.

Anxiety and depression is my story, just like cutting or anorexia may be your story. Only through talking about the issues can we take these stories and use them to inspire others that healing and forward movement is possible.

Occasionally, I hear Sanctus Real's song "I'm Not Alright" and wonder how many of us feel the same way.

> If weakness is a wound that no one wants to speak of
> Then "cool" is just how far we have to fall
> And I am not immune, I only want to be loved
> But I feel safe behind the firewall
>
> Can I lose my need to impress?
> If you want the truth I need to confess
>
> I'm not alright, I'm broken inside, broken inside
> And all I go through, it leads me to You, it leads me to You[87]

Do you feel alone? Do you feel like life is just passing by as you look on like an innocent bystander waiting to jump into the action going on around you? John Mayer's song "Age Of Worry" speaks to the feelings that come from anxiety in our lives.

> Close your eyes and clone yourself
> Build your heart and army
> To defend your innocence
> While you do everything wrong
>
> Don't be scared to walk alone
> Don't be scared to like it
> There's no time that you must be home
> So sleep where your darkness falls
>
> Alive in the age of worry
> Smile in the age of worry

---

87 Sanctus Real. "I'm Not Alright." Brentwood, TN: Sparrow Records, 2006.

Go wild in the age of worry
And sing Worry, why should I care?[88]

The message is all about breaking through anxiety so you can establish the person you're supposed to be.

As parents, we need to start asking our kids how they're doing. I don't mean the casual, surface-level question you ask every night after school: "How was your day?" I mean the heartfelt questions that penetrate our kids' hurt and expose their true feelings. They're living lives full of continual change and unexplained emotions, built upon social connections. When those connections begin to fray at the edges, their lives can unravel.

> Today's child has become the unwilling, unintended victim
> of overwhelming stress—the stress born of rapid, bewildering
> social change and constantly rising expectations.[89]

In late 2010, a young girl took her own life, bringing to light the fact that her parents had given her the drug talk and the sex talk, but they hadn't approached the subject of mental health.

> I wish we did talk about it before, but we just didn't think
> it was there, maybe because… didn't let us know that there were
> some deeper issues that were inside of her.[90]

Loneliness and desperation, when it comes to teen depression and suicide, can be difficult to deal with as parents because of the fact that our kids don't want to share these issues with anyone, including their

---

88 Mayer, John and Don Was. "Age of Worry." New York, NY: Columbia Records, 2012.

89 Clark, Chap and Steve Rabey. *When Kids Hurt: Help for Adults Navigating the Adolescent Maze* (Grand Rapids, MI: Baker, 2009), p. 133.

90 CTV News. "Luke Richardson speaks out ahead of D.I.F.D. night." Date of Access: April 4, 2011 (http://ottawa.ctv.ca/servlet/an/local/CTVNews/20110225/OTT_Daron_110225/20110225/?hub=OttawaHome).

friends. Coping with is an unavoidable part of their developmental process.

It's important to note that when I talk about self-injury in the context of the Bible, I don't intent to suggest that suffering with self-injury (or suicidal thoughts) means you're automatically possessed by demons. There's one another church-sphere conversation that breaks my heart almost as much—the belief that Christians don't get depressed, or that they shouldn't get depressed ever. In *Christians Get Depressed Too*, David Murray addresses this issue at length.

> "But Christians don't get depressed!" How many times have you thought that, said that, or heard that? How many times have Christian pastors and counselors made this claim, or at least implied it? If it is true that Christians don't get depressed, it must either mean that the Christian suffering from depression is not truly depressed, or he is not a true Christian. But if the notion is false, what extra and unnecessary pain and guilt are heaped upon an already darkened mind and broken heart?[91]

I know many Christians friends within my own church community who have struggled with depression and anxiety. I am now one of them! To argue that Christians shouldn't feel that way is just plain wrong. The Bible is ripe with individuals who've been struck by depression.

Character	Verse
Moses	Numbers 11:14
Hannah	1 Samuel 1:7, 16
Jeremiah	Jeremiah 20:14–18

91 Murray, David P. *Christians Get Depressed Too: Hope and Help for Depressed People.* (Grand Rapids, MI: Reformation Heritage Books, 2010), Kindle edition.

Character	Verse
Elijah	1 Kings 19:1–18
Job	Job 6:2–3, 14; 7:11
Various Authors of Psalms	Psalm 42:1–3, 9; 88

Many books have helped my fight anxiety attacks since my personal struggle began. I was about to leave for Halifax for one of my first tours of speaking dates after the diagnosis when I found out my flight was delayed. I panicked. Would I get there on time? Was this a sign not to go? All sorts of negative thoughts ran through my head as I entered the fight or flight decision in front of me. I first decided on flight and started to walk out of the airport… but then I remembered some tricks I'd read about beating anxiety. The first was that if I suddenly found myself panicking, the best thing to do was sit down. So I found a gate with no plane scheduled to leave, which meant nobody was around. I sat down. At that point my hands were shaking, my forehead was perspiring, and I still wasn't sure what to do next. I was beginning to hyperventilate right there in the middle of the airport! The second thing I needed to do was breath, which seems simple enough until you realize that you actually aren't breathing correctly and struggle to catch your breath.

As I sat there, trying to regain my breath, I remembered that if there are a lot of people around you when you're experiencing anxiety, you should just begin to people watch. So, for the next thirty minutes I did nothing but watch people. Then, after a while, my stomach growled and I thought, *Hmm, I'm hungry.* I had done it. That day, I beat my anxiety. It was neither easy nor pain free, but I took control of my life in that moment. I could move on.

Throughout this process, I have wrestled with one question more any other: where did this come from? Is my trouble sleeping a result of my anxiety, or is my anxiety a result of not sleeping? Or is there something else I'm missing?

I've now realized that my lifestyle had become unsustainable.

In 2007, I started a program called Arrow Leadership. In the first year, I booked more than eighty speaking engagements. In the second year, that number increased. I have since graduated from Arrow in 2009, which I loved, and jumped right into my Master's degree at Wheaton Grad School in Chicago. I upped my number of speaking dates to over a hundred per year. By the last year of my degree, I was booking the most talks ever (approaching two hundred per year) while having three to four courses on the go each year. My commitments had begun to overtake my life.

As leaders and parents, we have an easier time saying yes than we do saying no. We want our kids involved in all their favourite activities, we want to be able to enjoy our own activities, and we want to continue pushing forward professionally all the while not realizing that our rest time is slowly being pushed off the calendar. We don't think about our souls longing for refreshing with God. In an article from the Toronto Star, psychiatry professor Bruce Ferguson, of the Hospital of Sick Children, points to a growing

> deficit of adults in children's lives—we work and commute longer hours and have less time with our kids to deal with their worries and reassure them. It's a stressful world. Kids need a lot of support.[92]

We have to take the time to maintain healthy schedules that leave time for family growth and open conversation. When our outside priorities take the place of family time, our kids suffer from the loss of guidance they need from us.

My life was spinning out of control. I can see it now, after having been forced to stop and reflect on everything that was expected of me

---

92 Toronto Star. "Mental health top issue facing schools, coalition says." Date of Access: January 2012 (http://www.thestar.com/parentcentral/education/schools%20and%20 resources/article/1001024--mental-health-top-issue-facing-schools-coalition-says).

and that I expected of myself. I was living on adrenaline, which led me toward stress, fatigue, and eventually a burnout.

I've started to formulate a plan for the next eight to nine years of my life, a plan which will cover me until my kids are done high school and hopefully move into their university or college years. This plan will help me deal with my anxiety, allowing me to live a more balanced life. I'll begin to look more carefully at how I book my speaking dates. I'll still tour, but I'll think long and hard before booking fourteen speaking dates in one week followed by sixteen speaking engagements the week after. When I booked that type of schedule this year, I was thinking about my school bills and how I would pay them off.

My goal is to live a life that's sustainable, that doesn't increase my anxiety issues. A life that allows me to push past my anxiety into a life that's manageable and honouring to God. One of the big things I've learned through all this is the degree to which one's community can help. I have witnessed my church, my friends, and people who follow me on social media rally behind me, send emails, and engage me in meaningful conversations about how they can support me and my family through this time.

As a parent, depression and anxiety is a difficult situation to address in our own lives. Pointing out healthy developmental cycles and changes from actual depressed feelings can pose a challenge. Here are some of the symptoms to look for at home:

> A child with depression may pretend to be sick, refuse to go to school, cling to a parent, or worry that a parent may die. Older children may sulk, get into trouble at school, be negative and irritable, and feel misunderstood. Because these signs may be viewed as normal mood swings typical of children as they move through developmental stages, it may be difficult to accurately diagnose a young person with depression.[93]

93 National Institute of Mental Health "Depression." Date of Access: June 22, 2012 (http://www.nimh.nih.gov/health/publications/depression/complete-index.shtml#pub4).

I tell parents that the best way to address this in the home is to keep an open dialogue between parent and child.

I received the following email from a struggling teenager. I wonder how the emotions stemming from a grandmother's death might have been addressed had there been an aura of openness in the home.

> I was in seventh grade when I started getting depressed. People didn't like me, for what reasons they disliked me I still don't know. Life at home was getting bad. There were always arguments, and it was always me vs. everybody else. Into eighth grade, this continued... actually, it got worse. I was very depressed, and thought about suicide almost 24/7. Then my Grandma, the one I was closest to in my family, died. I was pushed farther to the edge. After one particularly bad day at school, when I was home by myself, I got a knife. I had the point against my chest, then I remembered something I'd heard about, something to help the horrible pain. I remembered about cutting. I cut myself on the lower part of my hand. It was short and thin, but it hurt... and that pain made me feel better.[94]

How is it that we are unable to recognize adolescent teen emotions? One way to think about them is to see them like the "X" on a treasure map. The emotions are there, clear and unmistakable, but the journey to understanding and coping with those emotions is full of intangible directions. The same way the treasure map guides you towards treasure through riddles and ridiculous walking instructions, so too is the journey to coping with depression. Some teens just cannot grasp how and why they feel the way they do. All they know is that they feel sad, depressed, alone, and forgotten. They'll look for anything to cope.

We need to start respecting the symptoms of depression by agreeing that we have to stop minimizing our teens' emotional states. They're not just grasping for attention. Psychologist Mark Schwartz makes a great point about respecting the symptoms of self-injury.

---

94 Your Story. "Looking for a Way." Date of Access: January 2012 (http://www.your-story.info/your-stories/2-cutting-a-similar/265-looking-for-a-way.html).

Mental health professionals haven't done a great job listening to the body… What they try to do is medicate the syndrome, call it a disease, cure it, get it under control, twelve step—anything but respect the syndrome and realize there's a … good reason that person feels and acts this way….

The very basis of our approach is that the symptom has a function and a purpose as a form of communication… If you simply use the symptom as a window, you'll eventually find out what happened to the person and be able to relieve them of that symptom. As soon as the brain is able to talk about it and process the traumatic event, the person is no longer doomed to replay it.[95]

Do we see our children's symptoms as windows into their lives? Do we use those symptoms as excuses for their behaviour?

Until we see the symptoms of anxiety and depression as windows into our children's true feelings and actions, we will continue to send them on treasure hunts to understanding their emotions.

Here are some detailed warning sings to look for at home in regards to depression and suicide.
- Withdrawal from family and friends, part-time jobs, and a loss of interest in items that were previously enjoyed.
- Slipping grades and skipped classes, or problems concentrating.
- Reckless behaviour.
- New or increased self-harm behaviour.
- Increased aggression and conflict with others.
- Giving away their favourite possessions.
- Expressing feelings of depression, hopelessness, and helplessness.
- Changes in eating, sleeping, and personal hygiene habits.
- Frequent complaints about physical symptoms often related to emotions, such as stomach aches, headaches, and fatigue.
- Talk of death, or suicide. This could include jokes about suicide. [96]

95 Strong, Marilee. *A Bright Red Scream: Self-Mutilation and the Language of Pain.* (New York, NY: Viking, 1998), p. 162.
96 Royal Ottawa: Mental Health Centre. "Information for parents." Date of Access: April 5, 2011 (http://static.capitaltickets.ca/sens_foundation/documents/30153.SuicideHandoutParent.pdf).

Just as important as being aware of the warning signs of suicide and depression are the reactions and conversations we have with our kids. Our reactions to their feelings need to convey the importance of their feelings, but also the love and concern we have for their safety.

The conversation regarding stress, anxiety, and depression needs to be taken seriously in any activity in our lives, whether it's in school, traveling sports teams, or other scholastic clubs. These emotions can creep into our kids' lives based on the pressure they receive to succeed, continue to attend, or take part in something that's uncomfortable for them.

The Toronto Star recently wrote that better education regarding anxiety and depression is the number one issue facing schools in this day and age.[97]

---

97 Toronto Star. "Mental health top issue facing schools, coalition says." Date of Access: January 2012 (http://www.thestar.com/parentcentral/education/schools%20and%20 resources/article/1001024--mental-health-top-issue-facing-schools-coalition-says).

IN THE THERAPIST'S OFFICE
Session Nine: by Dr. Merry Lin

IT'S BEEN AN INTERESTING WEEK. YOU FEEL LIKE YOU'RE STARTING TO SEE THE light at the end of the tunnel. You don't feel quite so alone, especially since you were able to email your shrink throughout the week whenever your emotions got out of control. She has promised to always read your emails, even if she doesn't have time to respond. Just knowing that she was listening to you made you feel better this week. You still had moments of desperation, but you've been practicing your grounding techniques; they have been helping, especially the Safe Place exercise, your favourite one.

Today, I come out of my office especially glad to see you. Boy, am I ever proud of you! What an incredible breakthrough you've made. I am so humbled by your trust in me, as well as your courage to open up and share your heart with me. I smile at you and your eyes have a sparkle in them that I haven't seen before.

You follow me into my office, and as we sit down I mention that I did read all of your emails. I am so glad that you're taking the time to really think about and process your story. I also thank you for opening up to me. I say that I'm very proud of you and the courage you have shown so far.

It's funny; you've never had an adult tell you they're proud of you. It makes you feel kind of funny inside. You like how that feels, so you smile at her and nod. You listen intently as she tells you that what you went through as a little girl with your older brother is trauma and that some of the struggles you've had are post-traumatic symptoms. She talks for a while about trauma and how memories can get locked into your brain and pushed out of conscious thought. Yet when things happen in life to trigger those memories, the emotions flood back in, overwhelming you. She tells you that the emotional part of your brain can "hijack" the logical part of your brain, that the thinking part of your brain can shut down and not allow you to properly "digest" the trauma of what happened to you. As she keeps talking about trauma and how it affects people, it totally makes sense to you. She could have been describing you as she was talking about trauma.

I can tell that you're resonating with what I'm saying, so I continue. I say that even though there are a lot of similarities with how everyone experiences trauma, there are also differences; no two people's healing journeys are exactly the same. I then tell you about a trauma recovery therapy technique I want to do with you called EMDR, or Eye Movement Desensitization Re-processing. I can tell you're confused by the name, so I laughingly tell you that it really is a ridiculous name and even the originator of the technique wished she had called it something else! But the name has stuck. Nevertheless, it's a highly effective method of processing trauma. It was initially used with war veterans, but then found to be very effective with all sorts of traumas.

I explain to you that EMDR works on the premise of bi-lateral brain stimulation, which basically means that the technique attempts to keep both the logical and emotional parts of the brain engaged while a person processes a traumatic memory. Since part of what prevents someone from properly digesting a traumatic event is that the logical part of their brain shuts down, it's important to keep that part of the brain engaged. I tell you that we don't totally understand why it works so well, but the theory is that it's kind of like the REM (Rapid Eye Movement) that happens when you dream.

I assure you that you'll remain in control of the processing, that it's like having the remote that controls whether you want to fast forward, pause, or watch the movie of the traumatic event. The goal of EMDR is to bring your emotional distress right down to zero, where you feel neutral whenever you think about the traumatic memory, where your body is able to come to a complete state of relaxation. I give you the homework of googling EMDR and then suggest that you can email me during the week if you have additional questions about it.

I then tell you that I want to take a trauma history of your whole life and get you to rate your degree of distress when you think about various events. That will act like a road map for us so that we can figure out where we're going. I tell you to rate the distress on a scale from zero, meaning no distress at all, to ten, meaning extreme distress. I laughingly tell you that the scientific name for this scale is called SUDS, meaning "subjective units of distress." This is just a way for me to gauge the intensity of the trauma and whether your distress lessens as we process the trauma.

As you talk, you realize that you've had a lot of bad things happen to you. You never really put it all together. Your shrink leads you through the entire timeline of your life, from when you were conceived to now, and as you talk you feel all sorts of emotions burning in your gut. You're surprised at the intensity of the distress, but at the same time you're feeling comfortable talking to your shrink. You know she's helping you to get better.

You have never talked so much in your life about the stuff that has been hidden for so long, but the more you talk, the more you feel a weight lift off your shoulder, like you don't have to carry the family secrets anymore, like it's really not your fault or your responsibility to fix your family; it's just a bunch of crappy things that have happened to you. It's up to you to deal with them, since no one can do it for you. You listen as your shrink talks about the importance of taking charge of your own life and your emotions, that even as you were a victim of other people's harm and you had no control back then, you have control over your life now. This makes total sense; you are so tired of being a victim. You are ready to be free.

Yup, it's about time. Even as you feel anxious about doing the EMDR, you're looking forward to it because it feels good to actually be able to do something about the crap in your life. Yeah, maybe you cannot change what happened to you, but at least you can change how you feel about it now. As you listen to her talk about how changing the way you feel and the way you handle pain can change the way you handle life now and in the future, you feel really good... like you can have a say in your life and make better choices than your parents or brother did. You can also learn to say no to people who treat you badly in the future!

common metaphor for life goes like this: "My life is a DVD on pause." I get that email all the time, leading me to think that there must be something here other than coincidence. Why do so many of us think our lives are on pause?

I think it goes back to the idea of living a medicated life. We're so stuck in between what our actions are and the feelings they cause us that we don't know how to move forward. We're stuck on how to move past these feelings and solve our root issues. If we want to hit play, we need to work out these issues. We have to start dealing with our stories, our histories, which determine who we are and who we're going to be. It's imperative that we deal with them in a healthy way.

Sometimes, in order to get our lives back on track, we have to seek out professional help, whether that's a medical doctor or a trained counsellor. They can help us hit the play button in our lives. In terms of my own life, receiving medication has been an integral part of the healing process.

Getting practical, let's start with dealing with a major scene in your life. It could be your parents' divorce. Using that as an example, let's assume your feelings include sadness, extreme disappointment, and abandonment. To cope with these feelings, in the context of this book, you might try cutting yourself. A scene such as this one—divorce—cannot change. We'll continue to think about it throughout our lives, but we *can* change how we react to it. We can also change our coping mechanisms. If it takes counselling to do that, so be it; we can talk through our issues. That's a good start. That's forward movement.

We don't break habits easily, but we can replace one behaviour with another. This is called behaviour modification, and it can only happen though dealing with our histories and stories. We need to deal with the real issues behind our cutting, drinking, and anorexic behaviours. Until we do, we'll be stuck in the same habitual routines.

So, what do I mean by dealing with our stories? A number of years ago, three important people in my life passed away in less than a year. Anytime someone we know passes away, we experience feelings and emotions that affect how we move forward. Each of these three deaths was painful to deal with on its own, but put together, it became almost unbearable.

The passing of a great friend, Warren Parker, came as a surprise because of the nature of how it happened. A drunk driver killed him. I was the best man at his wedding. Finding out about his death was one of those moments when your life just starts to fall apart. After each loss, a feeling of incredible sadness and unbelievable anger sunk in, weaving together to form a weird new feeling. All I wanted was to get beyond it. Honestly, six beers would have helped anyone get beyond it, but for how long would that have worked? Maybe an hour, an hour of freedom, but then an hour later I'd be back in the same place with the same anger, the same sadness, never dealing with the issue.

How do we deal?

We deal by sitting down with a counsellor. Wherever I went after my friend's death, and everyone I met, seemed to be a counsellor. This went on for a couple of months. I would have these conversations over and over.

"What do you do?"

"I'm a counsellor."

"Really?"

ACTIONS

FEELINGS

YOUR STORY

I mean, come on, this was like the fifth counsellor I sat down on a plane next to. I began to have conversations with people I didn't even know who helped me walk through this pain.

The steps looked like this. First, deal with your root issue. So many of us have deep hurts at our core that we've never addressed. We need to deal with them before we can move forward.

Secondly, we need to learn how to deal with our feelings. I know that when I have a bad day, I exercise. I also use television and movies to relax. I can lose myself for a few moments in my favourite shows. What I do is different from what my wife does, which is different from what you will need to do. We all do different things to deal with our feelings. Learn what works best for you. Try writing down ten actions that help you deal with your feelings. Maybe it's reading, writing, or drawing. It could be watching TV, listening to the soothing voice of Frank Sinatra… it could be just about anything.

EXAMPLE: WATCH TV
1.
2.
3.
4.

5.
6.
7.
8.
9.
10.

What works for you?

You might want to keep this list readily available, so you can see which activities or hobbies help you relax, and even which ones haven't been cutting it lately. These relaxation aids will probably change from year to year. If we lose track of what works, we might fall back into believing all the negativity we're trying to push past.

We need to know what works for us, so that when these situations arise we know what to do with them.

According to Dr. Karyn Gordon, our lives are like a jar of feelings:

> I ask people to imagine that each of us has a jar where we keep all of our feelings. Whenever we experience a feeling, it goes into the jar. We cannot control the feelings that are collecting in the jar, but we can control how many stay in there.[98]

All day long, our feelings go in. Think about it.
You fail a test.
You break up.
You lose your job.

---

98 Gordon, Karyn. *Dr. Karyn's Guide to the Teen Years: Understanding and Parenting Your Teenager* (Toronto, ON: HarperCollins, 2008), p. 90.

You get promoted.

Someone around you loses his or her life.

You fight with your mom.

You don't get into university.

All these things cause feelings. What we usually do with our feelings is throw them into that jar and cap the lid as fast and as tight as we can.

When our jars get so full that they start to slip open, we have a problem. We call that frustration. We become frustrated because we cannot fit any more emotional baggage into our lives. Sometimes, to escape our emotions, we self-injure. We have sex. We do drugs. We cut. We try to escape the emotions and tensions in our lives. We start to believe the idea that fake intimacy is somehow better than utter loneliness. We try to put in one more feeling, thinking we can squeeze that jar shut, but it explodes all over the place. That accounts for those moments when we freak out about little things; they don't fit in the jar anymore.

I'm pretty sure we've all been there. After we realize what has happened, there's always a "sorry" to be said. We don't have a choice over the feelings, but we do have a choice over the lid.

Here's the hard part. It's so easy to just crank that lid closed, but it's uncomfortable to twist it open. When the jar is open, we have to deal with all that stuff in our life.

So, where do we go from here?

ELEVEN
Image of Christ

God created human beings; he created them godlike, reflecting God's nature. He created them male and female.
(Genesis 1:27)

   She laughed, pulling at my chubby cheeks, then pointing at the tightness of my size 12 shirt. I died inside as she laughed and invited the rest of the family to laugh with her.

   That's when anorexia found me. But not yet. Anorexia wanted to see the rest.[99]

   —Anna

It's important we all realize that our actions stem from our stories, our own histories. In turn, our own personal and deeply unique experiences create our stories. Our actions and behaviours tend to be shaped by our personal histories. Our histories begin with God, as we are told in Genesis. God created us in his image.

---

99 Your Story. "Losing Yourself." Date of Access: March 2012 (http://www.yourstory. info/your-stories/3-eating-disorders/276-losing-myself-.html).

God spoke: "Let us make human beings in our image, make them reflecting our nature so they can be responsible for the fish in the sea, the birds in the air, the cattle, and, yes, Earth itself, and every animal that moves on the face of Earth."
God created human beings; he created them godlike, reflecting God's nature. He created them male and female.
God blessed them: "Prosper! Reproduce! Fill Earth! Take charge!"
(Genesis 1:26–28)

Even after God finished making us in his image, he had one more blessing for us.

God looked over everything he had made; it was so good, so very good!
(Genesis 1:31, emphasis added)

What happened after that to brought so much hurt and pain into our lives if God made us good and in his image? It begins in Genesis 3.

The serpent told the Woman, "You won't die. God knows that the moment you eat from that tree, you'll see what's really going on. You'll be just like God, knowing everything, ranging all the way from good to evil."
When the Woman saw that the tree looked like good eating and real-ized what she would get out of it—she'd know everything!—she took and ate the fruit and then gave some to her husband, and he ate. Immediately the two of them did "see what's really going on"—saw themselves naked! They sewed fig leaves together as makeshift clothes for themselves.
(Genesis 3:4–7)

Because of this one decision, pain and death became a possibility for humanity. However, God's love for humanity didn't end with that decision, as Jesus would come to earth and shed his blood so that we could live eternally with our Father in heaven.

This is how much God loved the world: He gave his Son, his one and only Son. And this is why: so that no one need be destroyed; by believing in him, anyone can have a whole and lasting life. God didn't go to all the trouble of sending his Son merely to point an accusing finger, telling the world how bad it was. He came to help, to put the world right again. Anyone who trusts in him is acquitted; anyone who refuses to trust him has long since been under the death sentence without knowing it. And why? Because of that person's failure to believe in the one-of-a-kind Son of God when introduced to him. (John 3:16–18)

Since it was the Fall that introduced sin and pain into humanity, the easy answer for why there is self-injury in someone's life is that it is the direct work or Satan and his demons. However, the answer isn't that easy. Even though I have strong faith in God, I believe that telling someone all they need to do to be healed is pray to God for healing or the removal of demons from their lives… well, sure, that could work, because we serve a God who's capable of performing unexplainable miracles, but if the person dealing with self-injury doesn't want to break their destructive behaviour or deal with the hidden factors that cause them to injure themselves, they'll almost certainly return to the same destructive behaviours.

God tells us in Isaiah 1 that he doesn't care how destructive our lives have become; we can still come to him and even yell our pain at him in frustration, asking for a fresh start.

"Come. Sit down. Let's argue this out."
This is God's Message:
"If your sins are blood-red,
they'll be snow-white.
If they're red like crimson,
they'll be like wool.
If you'll willingly obey,
you'll feast like kings."
(Isaiah 1:18–19)

If a person prays for healing without dealing with their background issues, and healing doesn't occur, their faith could be shaken. Or they could come to believe that they aren't worth saving. If you're reading this and you aren't a Christian, you too can be a positive influence on people's lives by being supportive, a good listener, and someone who's willing to walk beside them as they seek recovery from the struggle of self-injury. We cannot address one issue without the other.

You may be wondering what the Bible says about self-injury and if there are any stories of self-injurers in the Bible. There is at least one story, and it's found in Mark 5.

As Jesus got out of the boat, a madman from the cemetery came up to him. He lived there among the tombs and graves. No one could restrain him—he couldn't be chained, couldn't be tied down. He had been tied up many times with chains and ropes, but he broke the chains, snapped the ropes. No one was strong enough to tame him. Night and day he roamed through the graves and the hills, screaming out and slashing himself with sharp stones.
(Mark 5:2–5)

This passage usually starts the debate that self-injury and demon possession go hand in hand. However, like many passages in the Bible, there is more to the story. What strikes me is that the man who lived in the cemetery was troubled, driven into exile, and left to wrestle with his demons. Jesus contradicted everyone and went to the man. He engaged him right where he was, listened to his pain, and healed him. Jesus didn't leave the hurting man to deal with his pain alone but went with him.

Anyone dealing with self-injury alone is prone to destructive behaviour, but when that same person is met with compassion, a listening heart, and is given a sense of safety, security and healing become better options.

Self-injury is defined as hurting ourselves in any way, shape, or form—usually to cope with overwhelming emotions that we don't know how to deal with. What does God have to say about our bodies and how he intended us to care for them? God tells us that we were created in his image. God also tells us that our bodies are his creation and are to be treated as if they are a temple—or, phrased differently, a home for him.

> *Or didn't you realize that your body is a sacred place, the place of*
> *the Holy Spirit? Don't you see that you can't live however you please,*
> *squandering what God paid such a high price for? The physical part*
> *of you is not some piece of property belonging to the spiritual part*
> *of you. God owns the whole works. So let people see God in and*
> *through your body.*
> (1 Corinthians 6:19–20)

I know people who pray the following Psalm when they struggle with thoughts of self-injury. They use this passage as a reminder that their bodies are living testaments to God's work here on earth, that their bodies are worth everything in God's eyes.

> *God, investigate my life;*
> *get all the facts firsthand.*
> *I'm an open book to you;*
> *even from a distance, you know what I'm thinking.*
> *You know when I leave and when I get back;*
> *I'm never out of your sight.*
> *You know everything I'm going to say*
> *before I start the first sentence…*
> *Oh yes, you shaped me first inside, then out;*
> *you formed me in my mother's womb.*
> *I thank you, High God—you're breathtaking!*
> *Body and soul, I am marvelously made!*
> *I worship in adoration—what a creation!*
> *You know me inside and out,*
> *you know every bone in my body;*
> *You know exactly how I was made, bit by bit,*
> *how I was sculpted from nothing into something.*
> *Like an open book, you watched me grow from conception to birth;*
> *all the stages of my life were spread out before you,*

The days of my life all prepared
before I'd even lived one day.
(Psalm 139:1–4, 13–16)

There's no question that there are spiritual forces at work everyday. Paul tells us in Ephesians 6 that we have to fight to make it through life. He also gives us some great tools to help us get through the pain inside us.

And that about wraps it up. God is strong, and he wants you strong. So take everything the Master has set out for you, well-made weapons of the best materials. And put them to use so you will be able to stand up to everything the Devil throws your way. This is no afternoon athletic contest that we'll walk away from and forget about in a couple of hours. This is for keeps, a life-or-death fight to the finish against the Devil and all his angels.
Be prepared. You're up against far more than you can handle on your own. Take all the help you can get, every weapon God has issued, so that when it's all over but the shouting you'll still be on your feet. Truth, righteousness, peace, faith, and salvation are more than words. Learn how to apply them. You'll need them throughout your life. God's Word is an indispensable *weapon.*
(Ephesians 6:10–16)

Did you catch those words? Truth. Righteousness. Peace. Faith. Salvation.

As Christians, we're warned that while we will have to battle with powers and spirits that are not of this world, but we also need to be careful that we don't label our struggles solely as spiritual battles. Neil T. Anderson, in his book *The Bondage Breaker*, says that although spiritual forces can be a part of self-harm, it's not the only force we'll have to deal with in the recovery process.

To be effective Christian counsellors, we have to learn to distinguish between organic or psychological mental illness and a spiritual battle for the mind… Depression is a body, soul, and spirit problem that requires a balanced body, soul, and spirit answer…

There is no inner conflict which is not psychological, because there is never a time when your mind, emotions, and will are not involved. Similarly, there is no problem which is not spiritual. There is no time when God is not present.[100]

Regarding issues that involve the care and safety of our souls, we are reassured in 2 Corinthians that the trials that we work through today, such as self-injury, are not eternal issues in God's eye. That means we can win the battle.

So we're not giving up. How could we! Even though on the outside it often looks like things are falling apart on us, on the inside, where God is making new life, not a day goes by without his unfolding grace. These hard times are small potatoes compared to the coming good times, the lavish celebration prepared for us. There's far more here than meets the eye. The things we see now are here today, gone tomorrow. But the things we can't see now will last forever.
(2 Corinthians 4:16–18)

We were told in the earlier passage from Ephesians that God gave us the tools we need to protect ourselves from the hard times written of here in 2 Corinthians. We often refer to these tools as the "armour of God."

Stand therefore, having fastened on the belt of truth, and having put on the breastplate of righteousness, and, as shoes for your feet, having put on the readiness given by the gospel of peace. In all circumstances take up the shield of faith, with which you can extinguish all the flaming darts of the evil one; and take the helmet of salvation, and the sword of the Spirit, which is the word of God,

---

100 Anderson, Neil T. *The Bondage Breaker* (Eugene, OR: Harvest House Publishers, 1990), p. 21.

*praying at all times in the Spirit, with all prayer and supplication.
To that end keep alert with all perseverance…*
(Ephesians 6:14–18, ESV)

One of the most overlooked parts of that passage are final warnings from Paul to keep praying at all times, because Satan will use every opportunity we give him to work his way back into our minds and pry at the self-injury triggers in our lives.

> Nor does the Bible refer to any time when it is safe to take off the armor of God. As long as we are living on planet earth, the possibility of being tempted, accused, or deceived is continuous. If we can accept that reasoning, we will stop polarizing toward medical answers only, or psychological answers only, or spiritual answers only.[101]

As pastors, counsellors, parents, friends, and individuals who are battling with self-injury, we need to see the big picture. Praying over the situation as a family, or praying for your friend, is a great thing, don't get me wrong, but when we tell someone we love that all they need to do is pray… well, that can be damaging to their recovery, and damaging to their faith. There are deep issues that come with self-injury, issues which need to be addressed out loud to family members and counsellors so that Satan cannot use his deceiving ways.

Satan is a deceiver and will deceive us into believing that the harm we do to ourselves can help ease the emotions and painful memories of our past, but that just isn't true. Psalms has many examples, as do other books of the Bible, of individuals who deal with self-injury and depression as growing opportunities in their relationship with Christ.

> The Psalms treat depression more realistically than many of today's popular books on Christianity and psychology. David and other psalmists often found themselves deeply depressed for

---

101 Anderson, Neil T. *The Bondage Breaker* (Eugene, OR: Harvest House Publishers, 1990), pp. 21–22.

various reasons. They did not, however, apologize for what they were feeling, nor did they confess it as sin. It was a legitimate part of their relationship with God. They interacted with Him through the context of their depression.[102]

As parents and leaders, we need to start praying over our homes so that it isn't Satan who controls the actions of our children. Our homes need to be havens of healing and comfort. The psalmist didn't question his closeness to God during his times of mental illness; rather, he saw them as opportunities to trust that God would bring him out of the darkness. Neil T. Anderson provides examples of such prayers which can be used as declarations for your home.

> Heavenly Father, I acknowledge that you are the Lord of heaven and earth. In Your sovereign power and love, You have given me all things to enjoy. Thank you for this place to live. I claim my home as a place of spiritual safety for me and my family, and ask for Your protection from all attacks of the enemy. As a child of God, raised up and seated with Christ in the heavenly places, I command every evil spirit claiming ground in this place, based on the activities of past or present occupants, including me, to leave and never return. I renounce all curses and spells directed against this place. I ask You, heavenly Father, to post Your holy, warring angels around this place to guard it from any and all attempts of the enemy to enter and disturb Your purposes for me and my family. I thank you, Lord, for doing this in the name of the Lord Jesus Christ. Amen.[103]

Many of my friends walk around their homes and pray this throughout the year. They don't want Satan working his deception into their families' daily lives and want to proclaim their home as a home for

---

102 Murray, David P. *Christians Get Depressed Too: Hope and Help for Depressed People.* (Grand Rapids, MI: Reformation Heritage Books, 2010), Kindle edition.

103 Anderson, Neil T. *The Bondage Breaker.* (Eugene, OR: Harvest House Publishers, 1990), p. 246.

God. I believe that self-injury can be a spiritual issue, but I also believe it has deep psychological roots. Prayer is a powerful thing in the life of a Christian, but too often we use Mark 5 as a way to justify self-injury as demon possession, which I don't believe is theologically correct. Marv Penner, in *Hope and Healing for Kids Who Cut*, touches on the spiritual issue of self-injury.

> Well, let's be careful we don't violate the basic laws of logic here. The fact that someone who was demon-possessed chose to harm themselves with sharp stones or knives by no means implies that all people who harm themselves are demon possessed. Given what we know about the Enemy of our souls, it's not a stretch to think that he might be involved in facilitating something as destructive as self-injury. But let's not assume these kids are possessed by Satan.[104]

To say that all kids who deal with self-injury are possessed is just wrong. The spiritual battle that both Marv and Paul talk about goes unacknowledged for many people everyday. Marv goes on to explain how he thinks self-injury is tied to Satan.

> The truth of the matter is that the Bible describes Satan and his helpers in much more generic terms—prowling, accusing, testing, opposing, lying, and generally making life miserable in every way they can. There is no question in my mind that the phenomenon of self-injury is tangled up in the day-to-day reality of spiritual warfare, and that appropriate spiritual responses must ultimately be part of a complete healing. But I believe it would be inappropriate to assume that every adolescent who self-injures is in need of an exorcism.[105]

---

104 Penner, Marv. *Hope and Healing for Kids Who Cut: Learning to Understand and Help Those Who Self-Injure.* (Grand Rapids, MI: Zondervan, 2008), p. 41.

105 Ibid.

Self-injury's spiritual question is a tricky one. As Christians, every issue of our life is a spiritual issue. We're also told that God answers prayer and can work miracles in our lives everyday. When we as leaders are approached by someone who's struggling with self-injury and respond with a simple "Pray about it," we aren't doing a good job as a leader. Stop being scared and jump into the deep issues with those who are struggling around you. Be the compassionate, caring, and listening individual they need. You wouldn't tell a student who fell and broke his leg to pray about and it will be gone, so stop telling people to simply pray about their problems. That answer doesn't help them deal with their problems, and it doesn't help them grow in their faith. Self-injury is a spiritual issue, yes, but as leaders let's stop using fluffy spiritual answers as a way out of hard issues.

IN THE THERAPIST'S OFFICE
Session Ten: by Dr. Merry Lin

TODAY IS A DOUBLE SESSION BECAUSE YOUR SHRINK IS GOING TO DO THAT EMDR thing with you.

Eek.

But you've googled it a lot over the week and asked your shrink all sorts of questions. You think you're ready.

You know it'll likely take several sessions to process the full trauma of your history, as your shrink explained, but you're ready to deal with all your stuff. Nonetheless, you feel really nervous, because you don't know what to expect, even with all the research you did. You take a few deep breaths and fiddle with your cell phone, turning the music louder so you can't hear your own thoughts. You know you'll feel too stressed if you keep thinking about it.

As I come out of my office, I can see that you're a bundle of nerves. I smile at you and start chatting, to help you relax a bit. We spend a bit of time just catching up, and then I show you the EMDR equipment I have. I let you try the headphones, which emit beeps from ear to ear, and then you try the buzzers in your hands, which gently send a small buzz from hand to hand. I let you adjust the volume, intensity, and speed, so you can get used to all of that. You laugh as you feel the buzzers; they kind of tickle your hands. After playing with it for a few minutes, you choose the headphones. You like the rhythmic sound going back and forth from ear to ear. I explain to you that this allows for bilateral brain stimulation, but we need to keep the sound soft enough so that it stays in the background and doesn't interfere with what we're doing.

I explain to you everything that I'm going to do and say, then I ask you to take a deep breath and let it out. That breath will be my cue to turn off the beeps and allow you to tell me what you notice. I remind you that there's no right or wrong way to do this. The key thing is to allow your brain to do whatever it needs to do. To start off, I explain that you can choose whichever part of your story you want to start with, but that it seems that when you focus on the earliest traumatic memories and heal them, it seems to impact the later memories in a positive way. So, you decide to start with the memories with your brother when you were three years old; they seem to be the most distressing for you. I applaud your courage to jump right in, so we begin.

Your heart pounds as you lean back in the couch and close your eyes. You listen to your shrink's soft voice as she asks you to pick a snapshot moment of the traumatic memory, one that captures the most distressing part of the trauma. You think about it for a moment and a picture pops into your mind of your brother's face leaning over you. It's so clear; you can even smell his sweat. As she asks you to describe all that you see, hear, smell, feel, and even taste, you can feel the emotions rising up in you, emotions of terror, shame, confusion, and dirtiness. It's so painful that you tell her your SUDS right now is about ten. She also asks you to do a body scan and let her know where you feel the memory in your body. You notice tightness in your throat, heaviness in your chest, and a painful tight feeling in your private parts.

Tears roll down your cheeks, but you don't care; you're focused in on the moment. She then asks you to identify what you believe about yourself as you think of that picture.

"I am bad," you say. "It's my fault."

As you say that out loud, sobs burst from your chest, but you know you have to keep going. Your shrink asks you to consider the truth you would like to believe about yourself. As you think about it, you realize that you want to believe that it's *not* your fault. But that just doesn't feel true to you right now. Your shrink reassures you that the goal is to help you believe it so you can be free from the shame and guilt she says was never yours to carry.

My heart hurts for you, but I know we have to journey together through the painful parts of your story so you can be free. I want freedom so badly for you, because I can already see the beauty that's going to emerge from the ashes of your trauma. I know God has an amazing plan for your life and that it's through this hurt that you'll see his redemption, love, and grace. But right now, I'm focused on helping you through this very difficult moment.

I ask you to continue holding that snapshot picture in your mind. As you do, I let your brain go with it for about thirty seconds, watching your face while your brain processes it. I then ask you to take a deep breath and let it go. That's when I turn off the beeps.

When I ask you to tell me what you notice, you tell me that you feel the weight of his hands on your body and that your back hurts as it presses up against the bathtub. I encourage you to keep going with that. I turn the beeps back on for another set. On and on we continue, and as you work hard to process, I continue watching your face and body language to see how you're doing. I notice that the tension in your face seems to be lessening and the details you pull from the memory become more and more neutral.

I ask you to rate your SUDS right now. You pause, then tell me that it's at about four. I ask you what it will take to bring it down to a three. You say that you wish you had a protector, so I suggest that you ask Jesus to show you where he was during the traumatic memory.

Fresh tears roll down your face as you tell me that Jesus is right there holding you. While he's comforting you, he gently pushes your brother away. He's telling you how much he loves you and that none of this is your fault. You were just a little girl who trusted her brother and didn't have any control over what he did to you. You tell me that Jesus is now pulling you onto his lap. As you snuggle there, you feel a sense of peace. You know you're going to be okay. I know this is a key moment for you, so we continue to process through this for some time.

Jesus then shows you a snapshot of your brother being molested by a neighbour when he was just four years old, and you begin to understand the history of hurt that led to his bad choices. Your eyes snap open as you ask me whether this is really true. I tell you that EMDR processing is not always just about "factual" occurrences; without external validation, we cannot say for sure what is true and what isn't. I explain to you that trauma recovery work isn't about figuring out or proving the factual truth. It's about resolving the traumatic emotions associated with our memories. The brain often processes situations through the use of our imagination, so we can come to terms with our trauma. As an example, I tell you about another client who imagined herself kicking her abusive father (which she never did in real life), which gave her a feeling of strength, allowing her to let go of her feelings of powerlessness.

When I ask you again to rate your SUDS, you tell me that it's at a zero. I get you to do a body scan so we can process any of your body memories or tension spots. This takes a bit longer, and then I ask you to rate the truthfulness of the statement, "It is not my fault."

You're finally able to tell me that it feels completely true to you now. So I lead you through your Safe Place exercise, bringing you to a place of peace, relaxation, and safety once again. By the end of the session, I can tell that you're exhausted.

You can't believe how different you feel. You literally feel *nothing* when you think about the memory of your brother. Wow, this EMDR really works! You don't quite know what to think, since you're pretty bagged right now, but you know your shrink has promised that you can process it with her next week. In the meanwhile, there's an ice cream sundae with your name on it waiting when you get home. It's not the fix your mom wants it to be, but you know she means well, and you appreciate her for that. You also have some episodes of *Sponge Bob* waiting on the PVR .You plan to just veg out tonight and do nothing but watch TV and eat your sundae.

TWELVE
First Steps

W hat can we take away from this? I want you to read the lyrics to a song from Barlow called "Walk Away." To me, this song speaks about fulfilling these first steps. The first steps below are an invitation to you, the person struggling through self-injury, as well as those affected by someone who self-injures. Read these words and know that walking away from self-injury is a possibility.

> Christine's depression never seems to end,
> Cuz she'll never be as skinny as the girls on friends.
> She's got fat hips, and thin lips, she's jealous of a q-tip
> She'd take stupid over fat.
> She stuck her fingers down her throat for the very last time today,
> And she walked away…
>
> Doesn't matter that you're lying in the gutter.
> Doesn't matter that your brain's all cluttered.
> Doesn't matter that you're covered in scars.
> You're never in the gutter with your eyes on the stars.[106]

---

106 Barlow, Tom. "Walk Away." Toronto, ON: Sony, 2003.

These words echo what many of us long to hear, that we can walk away from the emotions, actions, and stories we feel are taking control of our lives. Someone else is in control of our lives, not our negative emotions, not the actions that hurt us physically and mentally. We have to make a choice about we want our stories to unfold. Are we willing to change? Are we willing to say, "God, you're in control"? Are we willing to take the first steps towards hope and healing with the help of friends, family, and God. Are we willing to make decisions that are going to affect us positively and move away from the decisions that have kept our lives on pause?

First Steps for People Struggling with Cutting and Similar

If you struggle with cutting, the first step is to ask yourself a question: are you ready to stop? If so, there are some accountability steps and guidelines you should place around you to make that choice easier.

First, find a support system of two to three people you can be open and honest with about your decision to get help, people who will stick with you through the ups and downs.

Second, make a list of tasks and activities that take your mind off self-injury, things you can lose yourself in. The list can also include a place to go that's away from your temptation to self-injure.

You need to get rid of harmful objects. You have to be ready to deal with

> I was cutting like crazy. I was addicted. But I got friends who helped. They guided me, and I am currently recovering from that life of cutting. It's possible to stop.
> Help does exist.
> -Anonymous

your feelings. That includes being uncomfortable, scared, and frustrated. I remember one girl talking to me about how these three feelings impacted her path to healing. I asked her how she felt at that moment. She paused, started to smile, and said "I feel uncomfortable, scared, and frustrated." You can feel uncomfortable, scared, and frustrated on the path to hope and healing, or you can feel uncomfortable, scared, and frustrated like you are now. You need to be ready to take the lid off your jar. You need to be ready to think about hurting yourself without actually hurting yourself. You need to put mind over matter.

However, none of these will work unless you can take one giant step towards healing. You have to want to.

If you struggle, you need to get some help. We call it therapy, or counselling, and it's not a negative thing. You can go to therapy either by yourself or with someone you trust and love. I know couples that go, and that includes high school through married couples. I cannot think of anything more beautiful in a relationship thea supporting each other when one or both are down.

Some of us need medication. Honestly, I think we throw medication around too liberally, but there are times when it's needed. Sometimes it's needed for a season, so we do it for a season.

There are also inpatient hospital programs that provide therapy sessions with a doctor, even counselling options that can help lead you on a path to recovery. There are twelve-step programs you can join as well.

First Steps for Friends and Family of People Struggling with Cutting and Similar

If you're one of those people who supports someone who self-injures, your question is: what can I do in this situation?

First and foremost, friends and family need to be confident in the sense that there is hope and healing on the horizon. A girl came to me once and told me that she went to her dad and told him that she was cutting. This was his response: "Wow, that sucks." Think about how that girl felt. She sat in front of me crying over her dad's reply. We can be confident and empathetic. Being empathetic means putting yourself in another person's shoes.

We need to be knowledgeable. If it means doing some research to understand the problem, do it. We also need to be knowledgeable about which indicators to look out for, because typically a self-injurer will go to extreme lengths to keep their struggle a secret. Whether it's through wearing long sleeve shirts, numerous bracelets, or even wristbands, these wardrobe choices are made so that the wounds and bandages remain hidden. Summer heat forces people to become creative to hide the scars. However, the choice to wear pants and long sleeves under a hot August sun is sometimes a good indication that there may be a deeper issue. Either that or they simply cut in other areas which remain hidden. Your son or daughter wearing short sleeves doesn't necessarily mean everything is okay.

The biggest thing is that we need to be optimistic. We need to be saying, "You can get through this, and I will be there with you as you do it." Can you say that? More importantly, can you do it?

First Steps for People Struggling with Suicide

For someone whose depression manifests through suicidal thoughts, the biggest thing you can do is talk to someone. This is life and death, and it is real. This is not a comic book or a game of Mario, where lives can be gained and lost continually.

If you're looking for help, you can start with your school counsellor. A guy once said to me, "I hate the counsellor." My response was, "Well, don't go to him. Go to somebody else." It's not like there's only one counsellor available. You can go to a private counsellor, or a private health care provider, or your doctor… and if you do not like your doctor, you can go to someone else. It might take you going to four or five counsellors to find the person who's a good fit for you. If your first counsellor isn't working, then find another. You can even call suicide prevention hotlines.

As a side note, if you're already depressed, don't add any more negative messages to your life. That includes movies, music, and friends. We all know that when we're depressed, all we want to do is curl up and listen to something that allows us to wallow in our own misery.

We don't need to do that.

Lots of bands trigger that, so just avoid them. You might spend a lot of time thinking about suicide when you're on our own. I would apologize for anyone who has ever told you, "When you meet Jesus, everything becomes rosy." That's nothing but a boldfaced lie.

Back in 2006, after speaking at a church, someone came up and asked how my year had been. My response was simple: "It sucked." They looked back with the blankest stare I've ever seen. 2006 was a challenging year! That guy had no clue how to respond to my honesty. Through my family, friends, and faith, I knew I could get through anything. I really leaned on all three in 2006.

The problem is that a lot of us don't have that option, so we turn to the media for guidance and comfort. A life that's grounded only in media isn't going to get better. I'm sorry, but it's not.

We need to start getting into each other's lives. What do you say when someone asks you how you're doing? We usually respond with a simple "Good." We lie through our teeth.

I'm so tired of regret. Regret drives me on a daily basis. I talk to people all the time who say, "I wish I got to talk to my mom" or "I wish I had talked to my daughter." So instead of always saying you wish you could do something, just do it. Start talking about the things you're uncomfortable with before it's too late. You only get one chance at life.

We need to stop having the boring discussions about nothing and get into the deep issues that drive our actions and feelings everyday.

We talk about community. Being in a community means getting into the deepest parts of people's lives and making an impact. How can we love our neighbours if we aren't willing to stick it out with them through the tough times? Real friends are friends through the good times and the bad. If someone in need approaches you and your response is to go away, what message does that send to the person looking for help? Does that promote your ancient faith worldview? Was that Jesus' response to those who came to him in need? Was that the attitude Jesus took to the cross?

Stand your ground, especially if you're a Christian. Explain that you might not understand what they're going through, or even understand their need to harm themselves, but that you'll be there for them. We need to start letting people know that we'll work through their problems with them. We need to be willing to see counsellors with them if that's what they want, or be available as accountability partners. We need to be there for them as they say, "I'm lost and don't know what to do."

Most people who come out of lives of self-injury usually note one person who never left their side. Marv Penner, in *Hope and Healing for Kids Who Cut*, challenges us to be that one person in the life of a young person they entrust their story to. We can be that person. We just need to be in the same room as them. I challenge you to start having real conversations with the people you go to school, church, and even work with. Stop having the whole "How are you? Fine. Good" conversations and start asking, "No, how are you really?" That's the only way to start promoting healing and hope to those around you.

First Steps for Friends and Family of People Struggling with Suicide

We must understand the risk factors. There are tons of risks, but without the risk there is little reward. The risk factors I'm talking about begin with knowing what's likely to increase a person's desire to hurt themself.

- Previous suicide attempts.
- History of mental disorders.
- History of substance or alcohol abuse.
- Local epidemics of suicidal activity.
- Family history of suicide.
- Feelings of hopelessness.
- Loss.
- Feelings of isolation.
- Feeling of being cut off from society.
- Persistent sadness.
- Complaint about being a bad person
- Verbal hints.
- Putting affairs in order.
- Happiness after a long period of depression.

I would also challenge you to google some of the other risk factors. I would rather question someone and be wrong than regret it afterwards.

How do we react to someone who's struggling with suicidal thoughts? You're going to realize that many of the steps are just the same as someone who deals with cutting, or any other form of self-injury. You need to be confident, empathetic, understanding, knowledgeable, and optimistic.

First Steps for People Struggling with Eating Disorders

In *Anatomy of Anorexia*, Steven Levenkron begins with this:

To all those brave souls who have given up the only security they knew for a healthier, frightening, unfamiliar adventure— the quest for a richer life.[107]

His book is about hope and frustration, but the underlying message is that we're going to get through it together.

It all starts with talking with someone. Eating disorders are life-threatening problems that need to be addressed. The good news is that you can get beyond them. Dozens of people have written me e-mails about how they deal with eating disorders on their own. They don't want to tell their parents. Each time, I tell them that if they could solve the problem on their own, they would have done it already. Who would ever be able to deal with an eating disorder while struggling with it on a daily basis?

> So if you are going through anything, please tell someone. Don't let it get to the point where you barely feel anything, like I did. The best thing you can do is talk to someone even if you think they'll judge you. If you can trust them then they won't. Don't keep it bottled inside until you burst.
> -Kailyn

If you fear that you're struggling with an eating disorder, one of the first steps to moving forward is admitting to someone you trust that you need help. Making yourself vulnerable and opening up about issues such as how you view yourself is scary, but those you trust can help elevate how you view yourself. They will be the ones to walk beside you and hold your hand as you begin to smile back at the person you see in the mirror.

Opening yourself up to the fact that you have a problem is a good starting point, but as you become honest with yourself you'll have to ask yourself a hard question: what are you emotionally avoiding in your life that drove you to anorexic or bulimic tendencies?

You'll also want to find yourself someone who can listen and help you move forward. Friends and family can be good listeners, but you need to know that they aren't trained therapists and counsellors. They might be the people you trust the most with your darkest secrets, but you

107 Levenkron, Steven. *Anatomy of Anorexia*. (New York, NY: W.W. Norton, 2000), p i.

need to realize that your friends cannot be your only outlet for dealing with all the emotional baggage that has built up due to self-injury. Yes, they will be your biggest supporters and they will be a huge part in your recovery, but they won't be the ones to get to the root of your anorexic or bulimic behaviours.

If you really want to have success, you'll need to avoid the people, places, and media that trigger your eating disorder. If reading *Cosmo* gets you frustrated over what you see in the mirror, cancel your subscription. If food courts cause you to binge eat, avoid that section of the mall. If your friends are obsessed with the latest diet trend, keep your distance while you get your issue under control. Removing the little temptations from your daily routine is a great starting point to rebuilding how you answer the questions "Who am I, really?" and "Where does my value come from?"

Our self-image and self-worth need to be shaped by two people before we allow others to dictate how we feel about ourselves: God and you. Not your boyfriend, not your wife, not the friends who put you down. Self-worth and self-image come down to just that… your *self*.

FIRST STEPS FOR FAMILY AND FRIENDS OF PEOPLE STRUGGLING WITH EATING DISORDERS

If your approach to helping someone through an eating disorder is to simply watch what they eat and how they respond, you're probably not going to get to the deeper self-image issues. Helping someone through an eating disorder takes patience, love, and understanding. We need to understand that the issue is much bigger than food. We have to continue to show them support, even in the little successes along the way.

One way to help is to exhibit healthy eating habits and exercise routines, helping them build up their idea of self-image and self-worth. This includes refraining from making negative comments about your own body and how fatty the fries are that you ate at lunch.

We also cannot count every calorie for our friends. Meal times for people struggling with anorexia are stressful enough without them being hounded by their own support circle. Healing from and overcoming an eating disorder must start with the free will of the individual struggling through the issue. If they aren't fully committed, our efforts as family and friends will be in vain.

We can build our confidence by meeting with a nutritionist and learning about how to help build a healthy diet and implement it correctly.

One of the biggest threats to a relapse is an emotional outburst or threats made by those in the support circle when progress doesn't go as planned. This adds to a person's emotional distress and can create more negative emotions, hindering the growth of their self-image, causing the cycle or reboot all over again.

IN THE THERAPIST'S OFFICE

Session Eleven: by Dr. Merry Lin

YOU CAN'T BELIEVE HOW MUCH LIGHTER YOU FEEL THIS WEEK AND HOW MUCH more relaxed you are. It makes you realize how much tension you used to carry in your body. You also find yourself able to talk to God more and you don't think quite so much about cutting.

Who would have thought?

You know that your journey isn't over, but you feel so much better than you've felt in a long time. You feel a lot of hope for the future, which doesn't seem quite so dark now. You look forward to processing the EMDR with your shrink today. As you listen to the songs on your phone, you find yourself bouncing your foot to the beat of the music.

I come out of my office and you greet me with a wide smile. My heart warms and I feel so much joy to see how you're being transformed right in front of my eyes. You excitedly tell me about your week and I laugh with you as you share a story about your little brother.

I know that last week was pretty intense for you, so my plan is to help you process it even further. Afterward, we'll play a light-hearted game that will give you another chance to share. I ask you to tell me how you feel about last week, and you tell me that while it was super intense, it wasn't as bad as you thought it would be. We talk about how the fear of facing our pain and trauma is often worse than the reality, and how often we remain locked in unhealthy patterns because of fear. I also commend you for your courage and how this shows me your character and ability to persevere, which I know will help you get far in life.

You enjoy hearing your shrink encourage you, but you have a burning question causing you a lot of doubt. Nonetheless, you know you can trust her not to judge you. You ask her about the whole Jesus thing and why he didn't stop the abuse from happening in the first place. Why would he let it happen to you when he had the power to stop it?

She tells you that it's a very good question; it's actually a sign of your growing spiritual maturity that you're starting to wrestle with the tough questions of your faith. She talks about doubt being the flipside of faith. Churches that don't allow you to question things can cripple people's faith. She then shares with you a time when she had to really wrestle with God because she felt so abandoned by him during a tough time she went through.

Wow. You cannot believe she went through the same kind of doubts you're going through. She isn't telling you that you're going to hell for daring to question what the heck God is doing. It's also reassuring that she isn't giving you any rehearsed answers, or quoting passages from the Bible that just make you feel dumb for asking the questions in the first place.

She tells you that we need to face the tough stuff in our lives rather than pretend that everything is all hunky dory, but at the same time there does come a time when we have to accept that there aren't going to be answers to all our questions—at least, not on this side of heaven. That's kind of what faith is all about, believing that what God says in the Bible is true even when it doesn't *feel* true, and choosing to trust God even when everything seems stacked against him. That makes sense, but you're going to have to think about that a bit more.

She then pulls out a game board and four small balls, plus a bunch of cards. As she does, she explains the rules to you. She tells you that the purpose of the game is to try to come up with answers to problems that are presented in the game, and in the meanwhile reduce your stress level while you play. You feel a little silly at first, but then you start getting into it because she gets really goofy trying to juggle the balls. You can't help but laugh. You like that you get to talk about real life problems teens sometimes face and then try to figure out some good answers. It becomes kind of practical, actually. This is better than doing homework where you have to read stuff and then think really hard. This way, you feel like you're learning, but having fun at the same time.

I love to see you getting silly with me as our laughter grows louder and louder. I also love seeing you act your age for once, rather than having to carry the weight of the world on your shoulders. It's great to see you more light-hearted. I know you're going to be okay. More than okay. It has been amazing to watch you grow and overcome so much. I see you as an overcomer and can't wait to see what God is planning in and through your life.

You really rock.

THIRTEEN
More First Steps

FIRST STEPS FOR PEOPLE STRUGGLING WITH ALCOHOL AND DRUGS

First off, it's not about alcohol and drugs. Ask yourself one question: why? Why are you getting yourself high on meth? Why are you getting drunk every weekend? You're doing these things because of what's missing in your heart. Substances provide a coping mechanism to escape reality. So, if either you or someone you know develops a dependency, ask yourself what you're trying to replace.

Next, seek some help. We now have teen versions of Cocaine Anonymous and Alcohol Anonymous. The help is there, but first you need to be willing to ask yourself the tough questions.

Some of the more common warning signs of substance abuse may include:

- Repeatedly neglecting your responsibilities at home, work, or school because of your drinking. For example, performing poorly at work, flunking classes, neglecting your kids, or skipping out on commitments because you're hung over.
- Using alcohol in situations where it's physically dangerous, such as drinking and driving, operating machinery while intoxicated, or mixing alcohol with prescription medication against doctor's orders.

- Experiencing repeated legal problems on account of your drinking. For example, getting arrested for driving under the influence or for drunk and disorderly conduct.
- Continuing to drink even though your alcohol use is causing problems in your relationships. Getting drunk with your buddies, for example, even though you know your wife will be very upset, or fighting with your family because they dislike how you act when you drink.
- Drinking as a way to relax or de-stress. Many drinking problems start when people use alcohol to self-soothe and relieve stress. Getting drunk after every stressful day, for example, or reaching for a bottle every time you have an argument with your spouse or boss.[108]

The best step you can take as a parent of a child you think might have a substance abuse problem is to talk to them. This doesn't mean running into their room yelling and threatening, but rather having a good honest conversation about the realities of the situation. As the parent, listening is the key.

It's also important to set clear boundaries about alcohol and substance use, boundaries which you talk about as a family. This could include a plan for parties for both the child and the parents. Some families I know set up a trust system, so that their child can call them at any point in the night to be picked up, no questions asked, if they see any illegal use of drugs, or underage drinking. However, there are consequences if the parents find out any of that activity occurred and they didn't receive a phone call.

As a parent, you can establish rules for when you're at parties, barbecues, work functions, or sporting events. These rules show your family that you take alcohol and drug use seriously.

---

108 Helpguide.org. "Alcoholism and Alcohol Abuse." Date of Access: August 13, 2012 (http://www.helpguide.org/mental/alcohol_abuse_alcoholism_signs_effects_treatment. htm).

First Steps for Friends and Family of People Struggling with
Drugs and Alcohol

If you're helping someone through a substance abuse problem, you
need to practice support and understanding. When someone we know
chooses to make a change to their lifestyle, we need to do whatever is
necessary to make that change as seamless as possible.

One of the changes may be helping that person decide who to spend
their time with. One of the biggest fears for anyone leaving behind a life
of substance abuse that they'll lose everyone they used to hang out with.
For progress to be made, there needs to be a support structure in place
that reaffirms healthy decisions that lower the possibility of a relapse.

> Admitting that there's a serious problem can be painful
> for the whole family, not just the alcohol abuser. But don't be
> ashamed. You're not alone. Alcoholism and alcohol abuse affects
> millions of families, from every social class, race, and culture.
> But there is help and support available for both you and your
> loved one.[109]

Helping someone we love with a substance issue may mean
suggesting and attending a support group in the beginning stages of
their recovery. I have one friend whose grandfather was a heavy drinker.
He was a member of Alcoholic Anonymous, and upon his grandfather's
death he placed the plaque in his bedroom as a reminder that even the
strongest of individuals needs a support system. That plaque had what is
called the "Serenity Prayer" written on it:

> God, give us grace to accept with serenity
> The things that cannot be changed,
> Courage to change the things
> which should be changed,
> and the Wisdom to distinguish
> the one from the other.
> Living one day at a time,

109 Ibid.

Enjoying one moment at a time,
Accepting hardship as a pathway to peace,
Taking, as Jesus did,
This sinful world as it is,
Not as I would have it,
Trusting that You will make all things right,
If I surrender to Your will,
So that I may be reasonably happy in this life,
And supremely happy with You forever in the next.
Amen.[110]

To him, his grandfather was one of his heroes, but he'd seen his grandfather struggle and wrestle through the recovery processes time after time. He also saw that whenever his grandfather felt alone, he fell back into his old ways. Even those people we think are mentally and emotionally secure need to have a proper support system when a complete lifestyle change is being undertaken. The Serenity Prayer reminds my friend that he cannot go through life's trials alone; he needs a strong support system around him.

However, there are also many things we can do wrong as friends and family:

- Don't attempt to punish, threaten, bribe, or preach.
- Don't try to be a martyr. Avoid emotional appeals that may only increase feelings of guilt and the compulsion to drink or use other drugs.
- Don't cover up or make excuses for the alcoholic or problem drinker or shield them from the realistic consequences of their behaviour.
- Don't take over their responsibilities, leaving them with no sense of importance or dignity.
- Don't hide or dump bottles, throw out drugs, or shelter them from situations where alcohol is present.

---

110 Addiction Rehab Now! "AA and The Alcoholic Anonymous Serenity Prayer." Date of Access: August 13, 2012 (http://addictionrehabnow.com/aa-alcoholic-anonymous-serenity-prayer/).

- Don't argue with the person when they are impaired.
- Don't try to drink along with the problem drinker.
- Above all, don't feel guilty or responsible for another's behaviour.[111]

Most of all, if you think someone you know might be going through a substance abuse problem, be ready to listen and walk beside them as they lean on you for the support they need.

First Steps for People Struggling with Anxiety and Depression
The first things I tell anyone who's dealing with anxiety or depression, whether they're the sufferer or they just know the sufferer, are the same. Be confident, empathetic, understanding, knowledgeable, and optimistic.

If you're struggling, be confident that you can get control of your thoughts when you become anxious. For me, I had to stop, breathe, and sit down. I watched people around me as I took the time needed to relax and regain control of my surroundings. That worked for me, but what works for you? We all need to find what works best for us to succeed in moving forward. If you're confident that you can regain control, it will be a whole lot easier to confide in someone about your feelings.

That first step cannot be ignored if you want to move past these feelings. You also need to disclose your condition to a counsellor, doctor, or psychiatrist so that the root of the depression can be addressed.

Here's what a one reader posted about their story:

> As a person that has dealt with cutting, depression and the thoughts of suicide, I urge you to get help. Not only will it benefit you but everyone around you. A common thought that is mistaken in your times of trouble is that no one notices. That's what I thought until my mom asked what was going on. This was before she was told but it was clear that she knew something was wrong.[112]

---

111 Ibid.

112 Your Story. "Erin's Story." Date of Access: March 2012 (http://www.yourstory.info/your-stories/2-cutting-a-similar/28-erins-story.html).

If you want to get beyond these negative feelings, another thing that has worked for me is running. Running isn't the solution, of course, but it's an activity I enjoy and it takes my mind off my troubles. The activities you once found fun and exciting will be effective tools in your arsenal to defeat depression. However, make sure you set realistic goals as you look for a solution. Thinking that the anxiety and depression will leave as soon as you begin an old hobby is unrealistic and will only cause you to be depressed over the lack of progression.

One of my favourite quotes about being confidant comes from Michael Landsburg, the sports reporter and host of *Off the Record*.

> When you tell people you suffer from depression, don't say it like you have something to be ashamed of... You have to say it with strength and conviction and a certain measure of confidence which you would say if you had something else.[113]

Don't be ashamed that you're hurting; be proud and confident in your decision to seek help and overcome the mental illness.

Becoming knowledgeable and understanding your anxiety and depression might just be your strongest tool in gaining the upper hand over your emotions. This will allow you to realize what triggers your anxiety and what causes you to feel low and withdrawn. If you find that particular individuals, such as friends or co-workers, trigger your anxiety, you might need to adjust your schedule at work or look at ways to move on in your friendships. The friends you have in your life are important, but your own mental health is much more important in the long term.

Be confident that you can overcome this.

Be empathetic to those who are trying to walk alongside you and who are supporting you.

Be understanding and knowledgeable in what you're going through, so that you can give counsellors and doctors the information they need to help.

---

113 The Saturday Ticket. "Michael Landsberg's Journey To 'Depression's Hell'" Date of Access: March 2012 (http://sports.sympatico.ca/home/thesaturdayticket/opinions/michael_landsbergs_journey_to_depressions_hell/7df64a9d).

Remember that optimistic and realistic goals are your greatest tools in breaking through your emotions. Addressing your root issues is integral for feeling better about yourself and the world you perceive around you.

First Steps for Friends and Family of People Struggling with Anxiety and Depression

If you know someone who's depressed, or who struggles with anxiety, know that you will be affected. One of the most important things you can do is help your friend or relative get a diagnosis. You may need to make an appointment and go with him or her to see the doctor. Encourage your loved one to stick through the treatment, or seek different treatment options if no improvement occurs, or if the symptoms intensify.

We also need to be empathetic to how they're coping and allow them to disclose information to you on their own terms. We cannot push them to disclose what they're either unable or unwilling to discuss. Too much pressure from the people they perceive as loving them will only drive them further into their own world and hinder their willingness to address the issues at the root of the depression and anxiety.

Also, be knowledgeable in the signs and symptoms of depression and anxiety, so that you don't make the mistake of dismissing emotional outbursts as "teenage drama." If there's ever any talk of suicide, or any hints at suicidal thoughts, be sure to address and report them to a counsellor or doctor.

Here are some suggestions for places you can go to for knowledge, treatment, and healing for mental health issues.

- Mental health specialists, such as psychiatrists, psychologists, social workers, or mental health counsellors.
- Health maintenance organizations.
- Community mental health centres.
- Hospital psychiatry departments and outpatient clinics.
- Mental health programs at universities or medical schools.
- Local hospital outpatient clinics.
- Family services, social agencies, or clergy.
- Peer support groups.

- Private clinics and facilities.
- Employee assistance programs.
- Local medical and/or psychiatric societies.

You can also check the phone book under "mental health," "health," "social services," "hotlines," or "physicians" for phone numbers and addresses. An emergency room doctor can also provide temporary help and tell you where and how to get further help.[114]

---

114 National Institute of Mental Health. "Depression." Date of Access: June 22, 2012 (http://www.nimh.nih.gov/health/publications/depression/complete-index.shtml#pub4).

IN THE THERAPIST'S OFFICE
Session Twelve: by Dr. Merry Lin

YOU SIT IN THE WAITING ROOM AND START THINKING ABOUT HOW YOU FELT when you first came to see your shrink. When you look back on the last few months, you cannot believe how far you've come. You've learned so much and you feel so much better about yourself. The main thing is you've developed more confidence in your ability to cope with stuff. You know that you still have a lot to learn, but you're totally up for it.

You look forward to seeing your shrink today because you want to tell her about the way you handled yourself when you found your mom drunk on the couch. Normally, you would have flipped and then the rest of your day would have been ruined, but this time you were able to step back and see that your mom has a problem and it's not your fault or your responsibility to fix it. So, you were able to take your brother to McDonalds for dinner and not worry about your mom, or feel like you have to take care of her. You feel kind of proud of yourself.

I come out of my office and greet you with a big smile. I'm so glad to see you! You've worked so hard over the last few months and I've seen such tremendous growth in you. I feel kind of sad because I know our time together is coming to an end. I'm super proud of you, though, and even more so when I hear you tell me what happened with your mom. I love when you put into practice what you've learned, and it's even more exciting to see you experience more and more freedom from all the stuff that really burdened you before.

Today, we do a review of all you've accomplished and how far you have come. We re-evaluate our therapy goals and see if there's anything else we need to do. Both of us agree that you're coping pretty well now, but that you would benefit from learning even more. I recommend that you attend a teen girls group that teaches life skills. We spend a few moments talking about what you would learn there and how great the support will be, especially when you're with other teen girls who have some of the same struggles as you and get what you're going through. I tell you that most participants find it very rewarding to be part of the group, as they don't feel so alone with their problems. You can talk openly and honestly with each other in a way you cannot do with friends or family.

I can tell that you feel anxious about attending this group, but as we talk it through, you agree to give it a try. I applaud your courage and remind you that I'll still be available to you for questions or ongoing support. We agree to meet once a month at this point, for me to check in on how you're doing and to give you a place to process things as you need it. I offer to meet more frequently if you encounter any tough times or need more support.

You cannot believe how sad you feel at the thought of not seeing your shrink every week, but at the same time you're ready to move on. You cannot believe how much you have come to depend on these sessions, even though it was like pulling teeth at the beginning. You're glad that she reminds you that you'll still have tough days ahead, and that you may have setbacks. That's okay. She tells you to think about how far you've come and not judge how well you're doing by how you're feeling in the moment. She reminds you that you can always give her a call or email her between our monthly sessions if you need to.

She ends the session by asking if she can pray for you. You feel a bit awkward, but sure, why not?

Boy, she sure doesn't pray like the preachers at your church! As you listen to her words, emotions bubble up inside you and you cannot believe the person she's describing and praying for is you. Wow, she's saying all these great things about you and praying for you in a way that makes you believe this great future really is possible.

You especially love the way she prays about Jesus' love for you and the way he views you as precious. You feel all warm inside and you sniffle back the tears. She prays all these blessings on you and then ends with a resounding amen. She gives you a big hug and tells you she'll see you in a month.

As you walk out the door, you feel like something is ending, but at the same time something else is beginning, something good. You don't know what, but for the first time in forever you actually find yourself looking forward to your life. Your friends have commented on you being different and you think you're going to tell them about how you've been in therapy and how much it has helped you. You especially think of Sarah, who's going through a tough time with her mom being sick in the hospital. Maybe she can get some help, too.

CONCLUSION:
Listen and Talk

W e've stopped listening and we've stopped talking. But we need to keep doing both. I want you to think about this quote from *Bodily Harm*:

Many teenagers are caught up with what is cool and with rebelling against their parents that it is hard for them to step back and recognize the truly important things in their lives.[115]

Would you say this is true?

Sometimes we forget what's important until it's too late. We need to take the time to step back and think about what we really care about in our lives. The things we need to care about are not the newest televisions or the newest video games; it's our friends, family, and faith.

This conversation is part of a journey. We'll all struggle with these issues in our lives. Some of us will struggle directly and some of us will need to be a support system for someone who struggles, but the fact is

---

115 Conterio, Karen, Wendy Lader, and Jennifer K. Bloom. *Bodily Harm: The Breakthrough Treatment Program for Self-Injurers* (New York, NY: Hyperion, 1998), pp. 30–31.

this will be a part of our stories. The choices we make will impact how our story will end. As we look back at our histories and stories, knowing where we want to go, we need to work on how we're going to get there.

Will we end our story in despair and regret, or will we end in the hope that we can move forward out of the wounding embrace of self-injury?

I once read the following statement:

> Although these people are sometimes called cutters—even in this book as quick shorthand—they are more than their disorder, their lives infinitely richer, their stories more complex, than that single label might indicate.[116]

Self-injury can include eating disorders like anorexia, bulimia, and binge eating. Self-injury can include cutting, suicide, and any other means by which we intentionally hurt our bodies. Self-injury can come from the way we deal with depression and anxiety. Self-injury *is* the conversation for today. Will we end our story in despair and regret, or will we end in the hope that we can move forward out of the wounding embrace of self-injury?

> Maybe redemption has stories to tell
> Maybe forgiveness is right where you fell
> Where can you run to escape from yourself?
> Where you gonna go?
> Where you gonna go?
> Salvation is here
> I dare you to move.[117]

Thinking back to the analogy of the feelings jar, you are left with two choices. You can let your feelings jar fill up time and time again

---

116 Strong, Marilee. *A Bright Red Scream: Self-Mutilation and the Langue of Pain* (New York, NY: Viking, 1998), p. xv.

117 Switchfoot. "Dare You to Move." New York, NY: Red Ink/Columbia, 2003.

and self-injure in any way you feel you have to in order to bring down your stress level. This will lead you further down the same dark journey you're already on. Instead, I dare you to open up your feelings jar and deal with what's inside. In the end, this will lead you down the path of hope and healing.

IN THE THERAPIST'S OFFICE
Bio

DR. MERRY LIN IS A REGISTERED CLINICAL PSYCHOLOGIST WITH OVER TWENTY years of experience in counselling individuals, couples, and families on a variety of personal issues. She currently works as the clinical director of a thriving practice in Ontario, Canada, providing Christian counselling and psychological services (www.lifecarecentres.com).

A frequent speaker at conferences, retreats, and workshops, Dr. Lin uses her personal and professional experiences to speak into the lives of her audience. She brings messages of hope and faith that help her listeners understand God's truth in very practical ways to transform their lives.

Dr. Lin is married with two children and is an active member of a local community church. When relaxing, she can be found curled up with a good book or spending time with her family. For more information about Dr. Lin, or to contact her, visit her website at www.drmerrylin.com.